Only One Life

A Biography of
Mabel Francis

Only One Life

A Biography of
Mabel Francis

by

Jean Vandevenne

CLC ✦ PUBLICATIONS
Fort Washington, Pennsylvania 19034

Published by CLC Publications

U.S.A.
P.O. Box 1449, Fort Washington, PA 19034

GREAT BRITAIN
51 The Dean, Alresford, Hants., SO24 9BJ

AUSTRALIA
P.O. Box 419M, Manunda QLD 4879

NEW ZEALAND
10 MacArthur Street, Feilding

ISBN 0-87508-667-5

". . . I live, yet not I, but Christ . . ." Galatians 2:20

Contents

Preface

THE FRANCIS FAMILY

MABEL FRANCIS was born July 26, 1880, in Cornish, New Hampshire. She died in Fort Myers, Florida, June 7, 1975. Family records show her first name as Rouchi, which may have been the surname of a friend or relative, and which apparently was rarely, if ever, used—except as an initial.

Her parents were married in 1869. The birthdate and birthplace of her father, Edward, are not known. He died in 1931. He was a minister and served churches in Massachusetts, New Hampshire and New York. He had six brothers who were also ministers. His father was a medical doctor. Mabel's mother, Martha Williams, was born in Potsdam, New York, in 1853 and died in 1921.

Mabel had three brothers and three sisters: George (1876–1928), Gertrude (1877–1957), Thomas (1882–1943), Susan (1884–1965), Anne (1890–1965) and Henry (1893–1961).

The Little Girl Who Hated to Dry the Dishes

T HE noon meal over, seven-year-old Mabel slipped out the back door. Gathering up her skirts, she ran as fast as her short legs could go across the yard and into the woods.

Safe! They couldn't find her here! Not with all the trees and bushes to hide behind.

She could hear faint sounds of activity across the yard in the house—dishes being scraped, the clatter of dishpans, voices.

And then the back door creaked open.

"Mabel! MABEL!"

Mabel put her hands over her ears to shut out the sound of her mother's voice.

"I know what she wants," the young runaway thought rebelliously. "She wants me to dry those dishes. And I'm not going to do it!"

When her father had announced one morning that drying the dishes was to be her job from then on, Mabel had felt sick. She hated drying dishes. Probably nobody in the whole village of Grafton, New Hampshire (maybe nobody in the whole world!), hated drying dishes more than Mabel Francis did.

Of course she realized that her mother needed help. Besides Mabel and her parents there were George (11), Gertrude (10), Tom (5), and Susan (3), all crowded into the parsonage. That many people made a lot of work, but it didn't make Mabel want to help by drying the dishes.

In a thick gray cloud of misery, Mabel sat on a tree stump wishing the mean, heavy feeling would go away. But she knew it wouldn't. Sooner or later she would have to go back to the house. If she went soon, the dishes, would be waiting for her. If she waited, somebody else—probably her mother—would have dried the dishes, and then Mabel would feel even worse. Probably in more ways than one!

The cloud was still there one evening not long after as Mabel sat in the big tent where her father was conducting special meetings.

People came from miles around by horse and buggy or wagon, and even on foot. The tent heaved and flapped as the evening breeze played on the canvas. Ordinarily Mabel would have enjoyed having church in a tent. If only she could get rid of that dark cloud.

At the close of the meeting, she watched as people crowded forward when her father gave the invitation to come and get right with God. They would get up from praying with their faces all bright and shining and tell what Jesus had done for them.

"I wonder," Mabel said to herself, "if I should go down and ask Jesus to help me with this dishes problem."

Finally she gathered up courage, slipped out of her seat, and made her way to the front of the tent. No one paid any attention as she knelt at the very end of the altar, but it wasn't just the pastor's little girl imitating the others. Mabel meant business with God.

"I'm in awful trouble," she prayed, tears streaming down her cheeks. "I just hate to dry dishes and every little while I run away. And I know it's bad. Please forgive me and please, oh, please, dear Lord, change my heart. Help me to like to dry dishes."

Whether or not Mabel was expecting one, a miracle happened that night. From that time on she actually liked to dry dishes. God had changed her heart!

The rest of the family noticed, too, even her father.

"Why Mabel," he said one day soon after, "you're such a good little girl lately. You don't make a fuss about doing the dishes anymore!"

Nothing could have made Mabel happier than to have her father notice the change in her.

Every day the Francis family gathered together to worship God. Father would lead in a song, read the Scriptures, and pray. Then everyone would join in the Lord's Prayer.

"Our house is certainly a safe house, with Father praying and Mother trusting the Lord," Mabel thought. "How can there be any safety for people who do not pray and trust God?"

Mabel's mother was quiet and gentle and

faithfully taught her children the things of God. Above all, she impressed upon them the deep need of people all around the world who had never heard of Jesus. She was especially concerned for the Japanese. It had been only thirty years or so since Japan had been open to contact with the outside world. The Japanese people had plenty of idols to worship, but they knew little or nothing of the one true God.

The Francis children had heard from their mother the story of Neesima Shimeta—a Japanese boy nicknamed Jo. Jo wanted more than anything in the world to learn about the God who created the heavens and the earth. So determined was he in his quest that at the risk of his life he became a stowaway on a ship and eventually ended up in America. Guided by God's unseen hand he came to know the creator God as his heavenly Father through Jesus Christ. Jo was educated in the United States and returned to Japan to establish Doshisha University in Kyoto, a Christian school for Japanese young people. But Japan needed many more Jo's to spread the good news of Jesus!

Often Mrs. Francis wept as she prayed for all those around the world who had never heard of Jesus.

"Don't cry, Mother," Mabel would console, "and don't worry. When I grow up, I will tell the world all about Jesus."

Mabel a missionary? That must have made Mabel's brothers and sisters smile. Even Mabel herself knew she wasn't exactly missionary material.

If there was a quarrel, she was usually right in the middle of it. It didn't take much to make her angry. Then watch out for flying sparks!

Every time, she would say to herself, "I won't get angry like that again." But the next thing she knew, somebody would do something to irritate her and there she was, popping off like a firecracker.

Finally, Mabel decided that she needed to be baptized. Maybe that would take care of her quick temper. Her father, whether or not he understood her reason for wanting to be baptized, gave his permission.

Soon after, Mabel was baptized in the river. Now, she thought, whenever she was tempted to get angry, she would think about going under the water, and she would never lose her temper again.

It didn't turn out that way.

About three days after her baptism, Mabel and her brother Tom had a terrible quarrel and she got as angry as ever.

"Oh," she thought in despair, "that's not it either. There must be something else that I don't know about."

And so she struggled on—trying to be good and not lose her temper, but often not succeeding.

2

The Teen Years

WHEN Mabel was fourteen, the Francises moved to New Hampton, New Hampshire. Now there were six other children in the family besides Mabel. New Hampton had a literary institute where the older children could go to school. It was very important to Mabel's parents that their children have a good education.

In their new home they became acquainted with a Christian family who seemed to know God in a way that Mabel had never seen.

It was hard to put into words: Christlike was a good one to start with . . . and joy . . . and love. This family seemed to be overflowing with joy and love. How did a person become like that? Mabel wondered.

Joy and love were in pretty short supply in her own life. And just at this time Mabel was becoming more and more aware of how far she was from being Christlike.

Her father had become very ill and her mother was occupied with nursing him back to health. Mabel had to look after her little sister and brother, Anne, age four, and Henry, not yet two.

This lively pair often exhaused Mabel's meager store of patience. She would tuck them into bed at night, all too conscious of the tangle of bad feelings that she had been helpless to prevent or unravel during the day. How she wished she could somehow erase the angry, unkind words and scoldings that caused the tears left on the cheeks of her little brother, even after he'd gone to sleep. Why couldn't she have been more loving? she wondered in anguish. But she didn't know how to change.

It was a happy day when Father was well again and Mabel no longer had to be nursemaid.

The longing deep inside her to live close to God only increased, however. One day, alone in her room, she prayed in desperation, "Lord, unless you give me assurance of a clean heart, I am never going to come out of this room."

Nothing between herself and her Savior: that was what she needed and wanted.

As she continued to pray and wait, it was as though someone put a hand on her shoulder and the Scripture came to her: "The blood of Jesus Christ, God's Son, cleanses us from all sin."

The blood of Jesus . . . cleanses from all sin! Yes, of course! It was done! Jesus had already done it. It was not Mabel who had to do it, it was Jesus. And He had already done it. She believed that with all her heart.

She came out of her room. But that was not the end of the matter.

Jesus' words to His disciples in the fourteenth chapter of the Gospel of John shed more light: "If ye love me, keep my commandments. And I will pray the Father and he shall give you another Comforter that he may abide with you forever. . . . If a man love me, he will keep my words; and my Father will love him and we will come unto him and make our abode with him."

Mabel knew Jesus was speaking about the Holy Spirit, whom God was to give to live within every believer as a comforter and helper after Jesus left this earth. She didn't know much about the Holy Spirit, but she could see from this scripture how very important obeying God was.

Obeying God. Mabel had never really thought about that before. She knew what *she* wanted, but she had never stopped to think about what GOD wanted.

Just what did God want? What did He want her to do? It would be easier to say yes, if she knew.

On the other hand, how could she say no to God? Did one say no to the God who made the universe? To the One who gave His Son to die for her sins?

Of course not! was the only answer Mabel could come up with.

So finally she said yes to God without knowing what He was going to ask of her. And God began to show her what He wanted her to do, little by little.

Before long she came to something hard.

Mabel's sister Gertrude, with her pink and white complexion and wavy blonde hair, caused the problem. People often remarked, "Isn't Mr. Francis's oldest daughter beautiful?" Nobody ever said anything about Mr. Francis's second daughter, Mabel, being beautiful, which bothered Mabel very much. She wanted to be beautiful, too.

Doing something about her stubborn, ordinary, straight brown hair would help. She had it cut in bangs and curled and primped and fussed, but just when she thought she finally had it looking pretty good, the weather turned rainy. Then her hair looked worse than ever.

Even when she was satisfied with her hair, there was the same old face underneath. Why couldn't she have been born beautiful like Gertrude?

One day God pointed out to Mabel that He had given her the face and the hair He wanted her to have, and she shouldn't be thinking that they weren't right. He had a plan for her life and He had made her just as she was for that purpose.

It wasn't that she heard the voice of God in her ears, but somehow, deep inside, she knew God was speaking to her.

"Put all that fussing aside and just be yourself." That was God's message.

"I do want to please You and obey You," Mabel said.

But one look in the mirror and she just couldn't bear giving up being beautiful. Or at least trying to be. Why, she wouldn't have a friend in the world, she was so ugly. She didn't want to be just plain old Mabel!

So began a struggle. Was she going to obey God, or was she going to spend her time and thoughts on the way she looked? She was so occupied with the problem that she couldn't even study. The question,

Are you going to obey God? kept coming between her eyes and the book she was supposed to be reading.

Obey God? Well, yes, but . . .

So it went until one day she was so upset that she couldn't even go to school.

Miserable, she lay on her bed trying to think the whole thing through.

She dragged herself to the mirror.

Oh, she couldn't look like that!

She went back to lie on the bed. She must obey God. She had to.

But how could she?

Back to the mirror she went. Then back to her bed. And back and forth. And back and forth.

At last she gave up the terrible struggle.

"Lord," Mabel said, "if every hair of my head falls out and I'm baldheaded, I'm going to follow You. Friends or no friends, I will follow You!"

That settled, Mabel made a surprising discovery: She didn't care that she wasn't beautiful. She really didn't care! Something wonderful had happened when she made up her mind to obey God, just as it had when she was a little girl and had brought her dish-drying problem to Him. When you say *yes* to God, the feelings that have all the time been saying no find themselves following right along and saying yes, too— just as the caboose follows the rest of the train.

God had something for her to do. He had told her that. She was part of His plan. The thought of living just to please herself became quite unbearable. She wanted more than anything else to please God.

Among the happy, memorable times during Mabel's teen years were the summertime family excursions to Old Orchard Camp in Maine. Old Orchard was a Bible and missionary conference directed by Dr. A. B. Simpson of the Christian and Missionary Alliance.

Unfortunately, the whole family couldn't go every year—there wasn't room in the horse-drawn carriage for everybody—but Mabel eagerly looked forward to the years when it was her turn to go.

The trip took two days; their old horse didn't know what hurry meant. Usually they visited overnight with friends on the way. Once at Old Orchard, they stayed the whole time camp was in session. Many people slept in tents but the Francises rented an upstairs room in one of the cottages on the grounds.

Meetings were held outdoors, and the audience sat on benches under the trees. Only once in Mabel's memory did it rain at the time of a scheduled service.

Everybody attended the same sessions; there was no special program for young people. Mabel sometimes got sleepy during the meetings, but she didn't let herself go to sleep. She didn't want to miss out on anything. Sometimes interesting and surprising things happened. Like the times when someone would be miraculously healed.

Not the least of the influence that Old Orchard Camp had on Mabel was Dr. Simpson himself. He was a large, broad-shouldered man, always immaculately dressed, but not necessarily in the latest fashion. One suit he wore was shiny almost to the point of being green—as black can get when it has been worn for a long time and pressed over and over.

Dr. Simpson didn't care about material things. He was all out for God. When he spoke, you knew you were in the presence of a man of God. He always seemed to have an audience with the King of kings. His voice was pleasing and melodious, and a sense of joy permeated the meetings. Often he would chuckle as he spoke of what God was doing, or was able to do in response to faith.

Some who came to Old Orchard traveled hundreds of miles just to participate in the missionary offering. Under Dr. Simpson's teaching, giving for missions was not a sacrifice, it was a privilege. He presented international missionary projects involving hundreds of thousands of dollars in such a way that people of ordinary means felt they could participate.

Sometimes women would take off the jewelry they were wearing and put it in the offering for missions. One woman gave all her jewelry and all her money. Then she shouted, "If the basket were larger, I would get in myself!"

Dr. Simpson was a man who could not rest until he felt that he was doing everything possible to bring Jesus Christ to the world. "On His heart, in His hands, at His feet, and at His command," was a saying of Dr. Simpson's that made a deep impression on Mabel.

3

The Call

THE house in New Hampton was a good-sized one—large enough to have extra rooms to rent out. One of the renters was a fine young man who had taught country school near the village of Tamworth. He and fifteen-year-old Mabel soon became friends, and before long, very good friends.

Unfortunately the young man was afflicted with tuberculosis. Unable to teach because of his illness, he suggested that Mabel take over his school. Though she felt unqualified, she decided to give it a try, and with the young man's help was able to carry on quite successfully.

Mabel's friend did not recover from his illness. One sad day he was buried in the little cemetery close by the school. Mabel could see his grave from her schoolroom window. Every day, despondent and feeling very sorry for herself, she visited the grave, leaving some little token of her love. Poor little schoolteacher!

One day God spoke to Mabel as she was visiting the grave. Here she was, the only one in the community who knew God. Why was she weeping over this young man who had gone to heaven? She must tell these people of God's love for them.

In response to that call, Mabel put aside her despondency and invited the community to come to the schoolhouse the next Sunday afternoon.

Since there was no other church service in the immediate area, nearly everyone came to the meeting, even some hard old farmers reeking of tobacco. So began regular church services in the little country school. As best she could, Mabel told the people of God's love and salvation through Jesus. Most of them listened eagerly and many turned to Christ.

News of the spiritual awakening soon reached the village of Tamworth itself. The minister there invited the girl preacher to give her testimony at his church.

Mabel went gladly and a spiritual awakening came to Tamworth, too.

After that came other opportunities all over the New Hampton area. Often Mabel's brother Tom, whom she had led to the Lord, went along to sing.

"You be Moody and I'll be Sankey," Tom said with a twinkle in his eye, having in mind the evangelist-singer team that was then traveling in the U.S. and abroad telling the good news of Christ.

Mabel's mother was somewhat uneasy about her young daughter-turned-preacher, but the Spirit of God was at work and lives were being changed wherever Mabel went. The messages she brought always highlighted the people's need to know Christ, revealed God's faithfulness, and made plain His wonderful plan of salvation.

All the while that Mabel was conducting these evangelistic meetings, her concern for missionary work was growing.

When she went to speak at a gathering in Haverhill, Massachusetts, she prayed, "O God, talk to the hearts of the people about missions, and let something really happen this time. Call someone out!"

That "someone" turned out to be Mabel Francis.

A missionary couple from Japan also spoke at that assembly. At the close, Mabel found herself at the altar among other seekers, desperately yearning for the will of God.

Suddenly, in a vision, she was surrounded by Japanese people. Jesus stood among them and said, "I love these people, but they've never heard of Me. I can't help them because they don't know Me. Will you go for Me and tell them of My love?"

Of course she would go. The impression of the great love of God for the Japanese people never left her from that day.

Her mother wept tears of joy when Mabel told her of the call.

"Oh, Mabel, you know how I love Japan, but I could never go myself," she said. "I am happy that you can go, and your being in Japan will be a great joy to me."

Then began nine years of experiences in preparation for missionary work in Japan. It was a time for more schooling, first of all.

She registered at the Gordon Bible School (now Gordon College and Seminary) in Boston. The school

was associated with the Clarendon Street Church
where her uncle, Dr. James Francis, well-known and
honored in Christian circles, was pastor.

One thing she had settled before she started
college: she would ask no one for financial help. Part
of her preparation to serve the Lord in Japan would
be to learn to trust Him now for her needs in America.

Mabel arrived in Boston with her finances on
shaky ground—only enough money for one week's
room rent.

That first week went by very rapidly. Mabel spent
a great deal of time in prayer and weeping (and
worrying), reminding the Lord of her very real need.
On Friday, just before the rent had to be paid—the
landlady had already mentioned it—a letter arrived
with $12.50 . . . just the amount needed.

"I don't know where you are now," the corre-
spondent wrote, "so I am sending this letter to your
father so he can forward it to you."

Mabel was torn between thankfulness and shame.
Here she had been carrying on in her prayers about
the rent coming due, when the Lord already had the
money in the mail and on the way.

"Lord," she said, "I have learned my lesson. I
am committed to trusting you for my needs every day,
and you know all about them. I promise that I will not
cry and fret again, as I have this week, about the rent
money."

That, however, was not the end of the testing of
Mabel's faith. There were days when she didn't have
what she really wanted—like sugar and salt to liven

up her menu of beans and cornmeal. But she was learning about joy and contentment in spite of short rations or flat-tasting beans and mush.

During an especially lean time Mabel was invited to a church in Brockton to preach. With the invitation came money for her train fare, with enough left over for a substantial meal. Her text for the sermon that Sunday: "Bread shall be given him, and his water shall be sure."

On this, her first visit to Brockton, Massachusetts —a shoe factory town—she quickly sensed the low tide of moral and spiritual conditions there. What a needy place it was! And God spoke to her very definitely, saying, "I want you to start a rescue mission for the streetwalkers in Brockton."

Me? Mabel Francis? A Bible school student, who had come to Brockton only to deliver a Sunday sermon? she questioned. Wouldn't there have to be some kind of a board or committee to back her up and provide funds?

Still, she felt she must obey the leading of the Lord.

Without sponsorship, she moved to Brockton and rented a storefront building that had a room at the back where she could live. So began a ministry in which many needy young women were rescued from drunkenness and immorality and came to know the love of God.

Who paid the rent? Why God, of course!

Through continual testing Mabel sought and found the Lord's direction for the ministries and the month-to-month needs of the mission.

One time at the end of the month, forty dollars was needed the next day to pay the rent. As Mabel brought this need before the Lord she had a vision of a horse shying away from something in the road. God spoke to her through the vision. "Why don't you just rest on My promises and really trust Me?" He asked. "You are shying away from trusting Me—just like that horse!"

So Mabel quit shying away and rested on God's promises. The forty dollars arrived from an unexpected source just in time.

In many ways, God graciously supplied the needs of the mission so that street girls might be brought to a life of respect and hope.

Often Mabel had to deal with evil men determined to snatch back the girls she had helped slip out of their clutches. Before this, her life had been sheltered. Now she was seeing firsthand the desperate need of sinful humans for the love and grace of God.

More and more Mabel drew close to her heavenly Father. Without even needing to think, it became the natural thing for her to ask God's guidance in her daily problems and to expect an answer. That answer would sometimes be so tangible that it was as if a human voice had spoken.

During the two years in Brockton, Mabel came into a rich friendship with Dr. and Mrs. Ira David. Dr. David at that time was pastor of the Alliance church in Brockton. The Davids were a great encouragement to Mabel in the mission work and in her spiritual preparation for her future missionary service in Japan.

At Old Orchard Camp the year Mabel was twenty-one, during the closing session a missionary showed pictures that included views of the Missionary Training Institute at Nyack, New York. The Institute, with its two-year course, had been founded some twenty years earlier by Dr. A. B. Simpson himself, and was being referred to by some as the "West Point of missions."

Strangely, it seemed that God was saying, "You should be going there."

Mabel didn't see how she could do that. After all, there was her responsibility for the mission at Brockton. Besides, where would the money come from?

After the meeting, on her way to catch the train to Brockton, she stopped at the pump for a drink of water.

A Mrs. Rose—Mabel didn't really know her, except for her name—was also at the pump and said to Mabel, "I've been watching you, and I think you ought to be in school at Nyack."

Mabel looked at her in surprise and had to confess what had just gone on between herself and the Lord during the meeting.

Mrs. Rose responded, "If God shows you clearly that you should go to Nyack, I want you to know that He has spoken to me, and I will pay your tuition."

Mabel had some thinking and praying to do on the way back to Brockton. If only going to Nyack were as simple as it sounded. But there was more to it than just having the tuition paid. For one thing, as much as she enjoyed the camp meetings at Old Orchard, she was not sure that the Alliance people were straight on certain teachings.

There was the matter of "holiness"—living a life pleasing to God. From her contact with certain teachers as a teenager, Mabel, contrary to Alliance teachings, believed that holiness came by the eradication of the old human nature—the self. Unfortunately, however, she had yet to see that happen in her own life.

She discussed with the Davids enrolling at Nyack and began to pray for direction regarding the future of the rescue mission.

Not surprisingly, the barriers to going to Nyack were taken care of, except for the holiness question. That she put on hold. At age 23, Mabel found herself at the Missionary Training Institute.

The course of study at that time for a woman planning to be a missionary included Bible courses, a language, History of Missions, Phonetics, Theology, Home Economics, Christian Education, Speech, Philosophy, and English Grammar and Literature.

As a student at Nyack, Mabel experienced the great revival which spread over the campus in those first years of the twentieth century. One time, for three weeks classes were suspended as the Spirit of God worked in the hearts and lives of the students. They found that little things—seemingly so small that they didn't matter—could hinder a close walk with God. Following many sessions of confession and restitution there came a tide of victory with—as Mabel was to describe it later—"songs and blessings poured out almost day and night."

After graduating from Nyack, Mabel felt the need to strengthen her academic work and so enrolled for further training at Defiance College in Ohio.

While at Defiance, seeking direction as to what mission to join when she went to Japan, Mabel wrote to a missionary who belonged to the denomination her father served.

"Do the missionaries stand squarely for the Bible?" she inquired.

"Some do and some don't. After all, who can tell what is truth?" came the answer.

This reply headed her in another direction: The Christian and Missionary Alliance. At age 28, with a good solid background of Bible training, academic studies and practical experience, Mabel told Dr. Simpson that she was ready to go to the foreign field, and that Japan was to be her field of service.

Now that Mabel felt it was God's time for her to go to Japan, it was as though an unseen hand took her financial affairs under control. Almost every letter she received had money in it. This went into the bank for train fare to Seattle and the steamship fare to Yokohama. Then it overflowed into the sum necessary in 1909 for a year's support in Japan.

Mabel Francis packed her little steamer trunk. Into it went her "missionary outfit," which included books, pictures and mementos of her family, a knife, fork and spoon, and three new gingham dresses which a lady in New Jersey had given her. Unfortunately, when she got to Japan she could not wear one of the dresses, a black and white check. In Japan black was suitable only for men.

She packed one little luxury, a half-pound package of Baker's cocoa. As she placed it in the bottom of her trunk she felt a thrust of regret, for she assumed that when that was gone in Japan it would be the last she would ever see. No one had ever said anything about a furlough that would bring her back for a visit to the States. As far as she was concerned, she was leaving home to go to Japan to spend the rest of her life.

Finally, one day in October 1909, the little steamer trunk was loaded into the buggy. Mabel's mother drove her to the train station at Westport, Massachusetts, to begin the long journey to Japan.

4

Japan

BEGINNING in the mid-1600s, Japan had deliberately shut itself off from the rest of the world. No one left Japan and no one entered. Death was promised for any foreigner, as well as the destruction of any ship approaching the shore. The only exception made was for Dutch traders at De-shima, far to the south, a small island in Nagasaki harbor. Survivors of an occasional shipwreck received harsh, humiliating treatment from Japanese authorities. Sometimes they were held like animals in cages for years. The lucky ones were eventually transferred to De-shima and allowed to return home on a Dutch ship.

By the mid-19th century, in the outside world increased American whaling, a growing American trade with China, and the constant lure of California gold created interest in a regular Canton-to-San Francisco run that would pass close to the Japanese archipelago.

In 1852 Commodore Matthew Perry was commissioned by the United States government to lead a naval force "to negotiate, conclude and sign" a treaty of friendship and commerce with Japan.

On March 31, 1854, Commodore Perry's mission was accomplished. The Treaty of Kanagawa was formally signed. The doors of Japan had opened at last to the outside world.

Now, fifty-five years later, Japan had still scarcely been touched by western civilization. There was little to remind Mabel of home when she stepped off the ship at Yokohama.

Everywhere were people, people, people, all wearing kimonos—the children's brightly colored— and wooden clogs which looked almost more like furniture than footwear.

But what struck the newly-arrived little missionary more than anything else was the hopelessness on the faces of the older people. They seemed to be looking out into space . . . which offered little but misery. How she longed to tell them the good news of Jesus Christ.

"God loves you!" she wanted to say. "Jesus has come to give you hope and joy and peace!"

But of course there was the matter of learning to speak the Japanese language. Until she had mastered that, she could only pray . . . and smile and trust that somehow God's love might shine through her, His servant.

When she arrived in Japan, Mabel knew just one missionary, Miss Christine Penrod, who ran a most effective rescue mission near the licensed prostitution area in Tokyo. Through the years, when she was home on furlough, she had visited Mabel's home church to tell of her work in Japan.

At first Mabel thought that perhaps God's plan for her was to join Miss Penrod in her work in Tokyo, and she even spent some time with her. It was a good and needy work, but Mabel did not feel that this was God's place for her.

Her work, she became convinced, was with the women who had not yet gone so far into sin. Better to go upstream and get hold of them, she thought. They needed the Lord as much as the prostitutes in Tokyo.

The work of the Christian and Missionary Alliance in Japan was very small in 1909—only two congregations, one in Nagoya and the other in Hiroshima. Mabel was sent to Hiroshima where she began language study.

She soon learned to live as the Japanese lived. Much of the time, especially in those early years, she lived in a Japanese home. Sometimes she had her own room, sometimes she didn't.

Japanese houses were small and fragile with sliding panels instead of windows and doors. Inside partitions were of paper.

The first sight to greet a visitor to a Japanese home would be a collection of clogs at the door. Not only was it impolite to wear shoes in the house, it would damage the floors.

Usually the only furniture was a low table for eating, with square, flat cushions to sit on. At night, thick comforters, called *futons*, were taken out of a closet and spread on the floor for sleeping.

A *hibachi*, a large pottery or metal pot, held a few

pieces of glowing charcoal for cooking and provided the only heat. In cold weather the family would crowd around the *hibachi* to take advantage of its warmth.

Learning Japanese was a struggle like nothing Mabel had ever before encountered, but it had to be done. She couldn't talk, read, or even understand when spoken to. It was like being a baby again, but with the added frustration of having an adult mind filled with ideas that needed to be expressed. Her ministry, her work for the Lord, was reduced to nothing; and so, too, it seemed, was the person she knew as Mabel Francis.

The Japanese language is among the world's most complex. The words have many syllables and a great variety of verb and adjective endings; sentences are long with a word order almost opposite to English; the meaning of a word is influenced by the accent—to name a few of its complexities.

A bright young Japanese girl, newly graduated from grammar school, was Mabel's teacher. She came at nine o'clock every morning and stayed until five in the afternoon. All day they worked together. When Mabel had learned a few words, she would try to put them into a sentence. Her young tutor would guess what she was trying to say and correct her if necessary. If the tutor guessed wrong, her pupil learned wrong. (Far more was involved in learning Japanese, Mabel was to learn, than replacing one vocabulary with another.)

Yet, through it all, Mabel found an unusual joy

as she reminded herself of the day when she could begin to communicate with the Japanese people.

Even before she knew much of the language, she tried to share the gospel with people she came in contact with.

While speaking to a group of women about the coming of Christ, she mentioned John the Baptist. "He lived on locusts and secrets," she later discovered she had said. The Japanese words for *honey* and *secrets* are very much alike. "Well, I was close, anyway!" she comforted herself.

At last the day came when she felt confident enough to preach her first sermon in Japanese.

The text she chose was Matthew 11:28: "Come unto me, all ye that labor and are heavy laden, and I will give you rest."

When it was all over, some boys in the group informed her that she had used the wrong ending on the verb and had said, "Come unto me . . . and I will give you *no* rest."

"But we understood what you meant!" the boys assured her.

Loving the Japanese people as she did, Mabel found it hard to realize in those early years that they were afraid of her as a foreigner. All foreigners were considered to be spies and were not to be trusted.

Even such an innocent thing as an object lesson for the children got the missionaries into trouble. To illustrate the love of God drawing people to the Savior, they used a magnet and nails. When the children went home and told the story to their parents, the parents were alarmed and angry.

"Nails, nails! That's it! Those are the nails they will use to hang you on the Christian cross!" they cried.

"This Christian religion doesn't agree with our national religion," the authorities warned.

Indeed it didn't! Mabel's heart ached for the spiritually hungry Japanese people whose land was actually littered with temples and shrines. Millions of people, especially in the lower classes, blindly worshipped all kinds of idols.

A man would go to the temple, toss a coin into a box, and ring a bell to wake up the bronze Buddha to ask advice in business transactions.

A mother would tie a cloth bib around the neck of a stone image to attempt to cure her child's cold or to protect the spirit of one who had died.

Worship of ancestors was the dominant force. Heroes of warfare were expected to gather annually at the Patriot's Shrine to give thanks to their ancestors for Japan's successes.

One of the notorious attractions of Japan was the legalized Yoshiwara prostitution district of metropolitan Tokyo where hundreds of girls were on exhibition in ornate cages, like animals.

In spite of the general opposition to foreigners, some people really wanted to listen to the Christian message. Often Mabel heard, "Hold on—that is too good to be true."

And she was only too glad to "hold on."

5

Finding the Lost

MABEL had been in Japan only ten months when
the missionary couple with whom she was
working went home on furlough. They had been
waiting for some time, and now they had a
replacement, albeit young and not very experienced.
So off they went, leaving the finances in the hands of a
Japanese man who had worked with them for some
time.

Unfortunately, and without anybody realizing it,
the man took advantage of his position of trust and
used some of the money for his own purposes.

When the missionaries returned from their
furlough, they sensed that something was wrong. There
seemed to be a barrier between them and this Japanese
man.

The problem, they decided, must be that he had
learned to work with the new missionary and liked
her better. Mabel would have to leave, for harmony
would never reign while she was around—"a man
cannot serve two masters," that was sure.

Well, then, she would go up to Tokyo to work,
Mabel said. But the senior missionary felt that she

should return to America, so—being the senior missionary—he bought her a ticket and put her on the next steamship headed for home.

Mabel was devastated. Everything within her rebelled against being sent home like this, but there was nothing she could do . . . except cry all the way to the States.

Upon arriving, Mabel went straight to Dr. Simpson, but the matter had already been resolved. The Japanese man had confessed his sin, and Dr. Simpson knew that Mabel had had nothing whatsoever to do with the problem. He was all for sending her back on the next ship, but in view of the situation he felt that it would be wiser to wait until several other missionaries were ready to return so she wouldn't be alone.

Finally, after about a year, Mabel was once more back in Japan. And how good it was to plunge into the work to which God had called her.

Reaching the Japanese for Christ during those early days involved traveling to rural communities and hiring a room in an inn or other public building. One could travel by train; Mabel, in the interest of economy, usually rode a bicycle. Once a room was found, she would let it be known when a meeting would be held. Many would come, probably out of curiosity to see what the foreigner had to say. Often there would be someone who was truly interested in the gospel and that person sometimes became the leader of the Christian work in that place. And so a church would be planted.

The first person to accept the Lord through Mabel's ministry was a young banker, Mr. Nishida. He listened attentively as she spoke and he stayed to talk afterward.

"My soul was so moved!" he exclaimed.

He began immediately to help with the ministry. Later his work took him to other locations, and if there was no Christian church when he arrived, he organized one before he left.

The second person to come to the Lord was a young girl, Asako, from a very high class family. She had graduated from school, she was lonely, and she didn't know what to do. "I want to know the meaning of life," she said to Mabel.

As Mabel shared the good news of Christ that day, Asako accepted Him as her Savior. For several years she lived with Mabel and helped in the work.

Another of the early converts was Mr. Ogata, a model young man who lived in Fukuyama and became the youngest postmaster Japan had ever had. During a devastating flood he had worked so hard that he finally collapsed on the street. Three of his vertebrae were just like jelly, the doctor told him. He was put into a plaster cast and given no hope for recovery.

Two young men who worked for him had become Christians and were determined to get him to the gospel services. By holding him up under his arms as he shuffled along in his cast, they accomplished their goal.

Noticing a Bible in front of him, Mr. Ogata picked it up. It was open to First Timothy, chapter 2, and he read, "For there is one God and one mediator between God and men, the man Christ Jesus."

"What a claim for these people to make!" Mr. Ogata said. "Why, we have thousands of gods! I would like to read this book."

Mabel didn't know who this gentlemen was, but she gladly loaned the Bible to him.

At the next special meeting Mr. Ogata appeared again, brought by his faithful Christian friends. This time the story Mabel told of the prodigal son and his loving and forgiving father made a deep impression on him.

He thought of his love for his own children, and he began to weep when he learned that there was a loving and forgiving God in heaven who loved him even more than the father in the story loved his wayward son.

Mr. Ogata went home that evening a new man in Christ.

"We could hardly keep up with him!" the two friends who had brought him exclaimed. He even forgot his cane, he was so happy. "Tonight I met my heavenly Father!" Mr. Ogata told his wife.

The wife thought to herself, "This is what the doctor said would happen—he has gone out of his mind!" She had married him after he was taken ill, and had never seen him with a smiling face.

The next morning, seeing him walking ably about, she thought, "It certainly gives him strength to be out of his mind."

Filled with this unaccustomed peace and joy, Mr.

Ogata went to the barber shop.

"I have found my heavenly Father!" he announced to the barber, accepting the hot towel the barber gave him. Not thinking, he stepped to the sink and stooped over to wash his face, which ordinarily would have caused him pain.

Suddenly he realized stooping hadn't hurt! When he got home he took off the cast, which was like a stiff corset, and bent in every direction. There was no pain at all!

He went to show the doctor the miraculous thing that had happened to him.

"What have you done to your body? That's not the same body you have been bringing in here!" the doctor exclaimed.

Mr. Ogata was healed! When it happened, he didn't know, but he was completely healed.

Jubilant, he went to work in Hiroshima, as head of the largest post office in that section.

Now, to his delight, he could make enough money to care for his family and have extra to support students who were studying to teach God's Word.

But God had other plans for Mr. Ogata: Go to school and prepare to preach.

His wife did not like that idea. After all, he had three daughters to marry off. That cost money.

"I have to obey God before everything else," he quietly answered.

Finally his wife agreed. "Why don't you go to school and obey God, and I will take care of the children," she said.

In those days, a Japanese gentleman did not do menial work, and Mr. Ogata was a gentleman. Gentlemen wore a certain kind of clogs and a certain kind of silk clothing. But gentleman or not, Mr. Ogata worked in the kitchen at the school and even did the buying, which was really humbling for a Japanese gentleman. He meant business for the Lord.

After some time, Mrs. Ogata came to Mabel and said, "You know, I have been reading the Bible and I have come upon a wonderful statement. It says, 'Come unto me, all ye that labor . . . and I will give you rest.' Now I was brought up in a Buddhist temple, and my father was a priest there. But who would dare to say a thing like that—'Come . . . and I will give you rest'?"

Mabel talked with her about Jesus and prayed with her. The next thing Mabel knew, Mrs. Ogata and the girls were at the school with Mr. Ogata.

Upon finishing school, Mr. Ogata went to Matsuyama to work with Mabel. He stepped out on faith, trusting God to take care of his needs and those of his family, even on the salary of a preacher—which in those days was very, very small compared to what he had been paid when he worked for the post office.

Because of Mr. Ogata's faithfulness, wisdom, and hard work, a new church was opened in that area every year. A quiet, retiring man who did not seek attention for himself, he was a great spiritual influence and became a leader of the Alliance work in Japan.

By the 1920s two more members of the Francis family had dedicated their lives to serve the Lord in

Japan: Tom—Mabel's childhood sparring partner and singing teammate when she was a girl preacher back in Tamworth, New Hampshire—and "little sister" Anne Dievendorf, by this time a widow. Both Tom and Anne taught in the mission Bible school, and Tom was active as an evangelist as well. How pleased their mother must have been.

6

A Parting of the Ways

ECONOMIC problems in the United States were bringing hard times in many sectors, even to missionary work abroad. In 1934, word came from the Foreign Department offices of the Alliance in New York that they felt it best to withdraw from Japan. Missionaries would be expected to come home, and—if possible—be assigned to another field.

Leave Japan! Suddenly Mabel's whole world was falling apart around her. She was alone at the time, Tom and his wife and Anne having returned to the States on furlough.

"What am I to do?" she asked herself over and over.

Still, since the Board was calling her home, what choice did she have? How could she stay in Japan? What would she do for money?

But how could she leave? She had come this far under divine command. What would become of God's work? The churches that were springing up as a result of her work needed her.

The pastors of the Japanese churches were also upset. How could they carry on without the missionaries? They wrote a letter to the mission board in America expressing their sorrow and dismay that the missionaries would be leaving.

The letter from the Board, however, was really an ultimatum. Decisions had already been made, and the withdrawal from Japan was already determined. Actually, there was nothing to talk about, no negotiations to be made.

Upstairs, the trunk that Mabel had brought to Japan stood empty. Nothing to do but start packing, but she just couldn't seem to make any progress. Dutifully, she would start up the stairs with something to put in the trunk, and her hands would drop at her sides.

"Oh, Lord, show me what to do!" she agonized.

She came home from calling one day, heavy-hearted, with *What shall I do?* repeating itself over and over in her mind.

Suddenly a voice spoke so distinctly that she thought she was hearing it with her natural ears. "Would you fear to stay here and just trust Me, even if the Board does let you off?"

She knew it was God speaking to her. Mabel looked up and said, "Lord, You know I have told You that I will do whatever You want."

Again the voice spoke. "You know that I have called you to Japan—that is even before the Board's call. And the work I wanted you to do is not yet finished. I want you to stay here."

The words struck fear in Mabel's heart. What of her future if she stayed in Japan with no home church or organization or board in back of her?

"Lord," Mabel said, "if I live to be seventy years old, everyone in America will forget that I exist, and I might starve right here."

"If I let you live to be seventy . . . ," the voice persisted.

That was a reminder that her life was completely in God's hands.

That settled it. "Heavenly Father," Mabel said, "I will stay here."

The burden and uncertainty lifted. Joy flooded over her. "Yes, yes, yes!" As she went out the next morning, it seemed that even her feet were singing in answer to the will of God.

The Alliance Board had its leading from the Lord, but so did missionary Mabel Francis. They were just not in the same direction.

So the mission pulled out of Japan, and Mabel stayed. Anne and Tom and his wife also chose to stay. As it turned out, the work, being God's work, continued to grow and thrive, mission or no mission.

7

Not I

"**I** WOULDN'T be anything but a missionary!" Mabel often thought, and sometimes said aloud. What was all the wealth of the world? Nothing, compared with the joy of seeing God do things for men and women and boys and girls that no one else could do!

But there was a blight on the landscape.

When Mabel was a student at Nyack, a guest missionary speaker made a statement in a chapel service that Mabel questioned at the time: "While you are in school and while you are at home, you are busy praying for others. When you get to the mission field, you will find that you will be often praying for yourself."

Now Mabel was beginning to realize that what the missionary had said was true. Yes, Mabel Francis needed prayer. She wasn't the victorious Christian she had thought she was. Oh, she had led a number of Japanese to the Lord, their lives had been changed, and that was wonderful; but what was going on in her own life wasn't wonderful at all.

Constantly she was seeing how unchristlike and full of self she was. She had thought that had all been dealt with long ago before she ever came to Japan, but now she knew better.

Jesus humbled Himself and became not just a man, but a servant, even to dying on the cross.

Humbled Himself! Mabel knew she had a lot to learn about humillty. According to the book by Andrew Murray that she was reading, humility is "never to be fretted, or vexed, or irritated, or sore, or disappointed."

When she read that she threw the book down.

"Lord," she wailed, "I just don't know anything about humility. I do get vexed. I get irritated. I get sore."

Mabel began seeking the Lord and searching with all her heart. Oh, for something special from the Lord! Something that would free her from the bondage of herself and fill her with a new power. Then she would be able to go out and really do things for the Lord.

It didn't happen.

On the contrary, it seemed that everything was closing in on her. Things bothered her—all the little irritations of everyday living. A dresser drawer that wouldn't go in straight, for example. She would get so aggravated that she felt like giving the thing a kick. She didn't, but she felt like it.

Everything in Japan—even the people—seemed to operate in slow motion. Nothing was ever done quickly. Greeting a friend on the street involved stopping and actually going through a little ceremony before you could continue on your way. Even opening a door had to be done in a certain way. And so it went.

Meanwhile, there was so much to be done for the Lord!

Her irritation was like a kettle of water sitting over a fire. As it gets hotter, the water begins to bubble a little, then more and more until it comes to a full boil. It may even boil over!

"Muko, MUKO, MUKO!" as the Japanese would say.

There was that elderly man who without fail would get up in a meeting and give a long testimony of how the Lord had so wonderfully saved him. It was true. He *had* been wonderfully saved! The problem was he didn't have any teeth and could not talk plainly. It was hard to understand him.

Mabel could not help but feel irritated every time he got up to give his testimony.

"Oh, Lord, stop him," she would pray. "He is spoiling the meeting. Everything will go to pieces here."

Then God spoke to Mabel: "I can bless right over that old man. He is standing there trying to glorify Me. But *you* do bother Me by sitting here and fretting over it."

Shame swept over her when she realized the sinfulness of her fretting spirit, which was crowding out the love of Christ that the Japanese so desperately needed to see.

And there was more. "Humility," Andrew Murray's book said, "is to wonder at nothing that is done to me. It is to feel no resentment against anybody or anything. It is to be at rest when nobody praises me, when I am blamed or suspected. It is to have a blessed home in the Lord, where we can go in and shut the door, and kneel to our Father in secret, and be at peace in the deep sea of calm when all around is in trouble."

"Lord Jesus, make that a reality in me. I must have it!" Mabel prayed. She most certainly did feel resentment. She was not at rest.

It wasn't easy to overlook the unappreciativeness of the Japanese. Here she had sacrificed and was living under hardship. She ate food she didn't really care for—she had never learned to really like Japanese food. She sat on the floor, which was certainly not comfortable to one used to sitting on a chair. She suffered from the cold in the winter, living in a drafty Japanese house. In really cold weather she had to wear her heavy winter coat inside, which made her shoulders ache. All to bring the Japanese the good news of Christ! Of course that was what she wanted to do. But did they appreciate it? No! They said, "Why did you come? We've got enough gods without your telling us about yours!"

Mabel had to spend a lot of time bicycling over rough, hilly roads. After a few miles of going up and down and sometimes landing *kerchunk!* in a pothole, she would feel as if she had had a good spanking. One day during an especially rough trip she pulled off to the side of the road and sat on a stone to cry. "How am I going to go on?" she asked herself as she sat there feeling sorry for herself.

Finally, Mabel decided she needed to take this matter to the Lord, as she had done when she was a little girl.

She discovered a germ of the answer in Galatians 2:20: "I am crucified with Christ. Nevertheless I live, yet not I, but Christ liveth in me."

Crucified with Christ. What did that mean? And there were such concepts as dying to self or denying self in other passages of Scripture. How did you die to yourself? Or deny yourself?

Somehow she needed to let Jesus Himself take over her life. Every nook and cranny. Not just what showed in church on Sundays when she was THE MISSIONARY.

During this period of time, Mabel lived in a big house and had several Japanese young women living with her. There was a lot of coming and going and she kept a pad of paper and a box of pencils by the front door for messages. She instructed the girls: If a pencil point should break, do not put the pencil back in the box, but lay it aside so it can be sharpened later. There was nothing more aggravating than picking up a broken pencil when she was in a hurry. The girls agreed to do as she asked.

One busy morning a man stopped by to leave an address. He was in a hurry to catch a train. Mabel took a pencil from the box. The lead was broken. She picked up another. This was broken, too. She picked up another, and another. The seventh was the last in the box, and it, too, was broken. Mabel threw it down in disgust.

"I told them not to put broken pencils back in the box!" she muttered angrily as she hurried off to find a pencil that would write.

Then a wave of shame swept over her. Oh, such impatience! Such an unchristlike attitude! It was self in control instead of Christ.

As soon as the visitor had gone, Mabel called the girls together.

"Girls," she said, "I have grieved the Holy Spirit! I want you to pray for me."

No doubt the girls looked at each other in puzzlement. Their beloved Sensei grieve the Holy Spirit? How could that be?

When Mabel related the incident, the girls insisted that they were to blame, not her. But Mabel in turn insisted that her impatient spirit far exceeded any wrong they had done, and it must be dealt with. She must bring it to the Lord. No excuses. Not, "I was impatient, but . . ." as she had said many times before. It was easy to put the blame on circumstances, or on somebody else.

Now, at last, Mabel gave her impatience over to the Lord, and that was the last she ever saw of it. Though there were many occasions after that to feel impatient, she never did.

Then there came a very deep trial. One of the missionary women gossiped about Mabel—she was not living "morally right," the woman said. There was not a bit of truth in what she said, but the word spread until it reached the mission board in the States. They decided to send a man to investigate.

"Oh, what shall I do?" Mabel agonized. God's answer to her was, "Don't say one word. Don't say anything to anybody. It is in My hands. I'll take care of it."

But that was easier said than done. How could she not respond to such treatment and defend herself? It was all so unfair! She wanted to fight back, to say *something!* At least one word to straighten this woman out.

The stress took its toll and Mabel actually became ill.

Anne said to her one day, "Oh, Mabel, you look so bad! Can't you go and get fixed up, somehow?"

"Just wait until I get through with this. I'll be all right," Mabel responded.

The man the Board sent from the States had been a classmate at Nyack. Though he didn't ask her directly, "Are you living in sin?" it was a humiliating experience to be the subject of such an investigation. Nevertheless she answered all his questions without letting on that she knew what he was trying to get at and defending herself.

After he had gone, Mabel wondered what would happen. Would she be called back to the States? But more than anything else, she wanted to have the right attitude. No matter about anybody else.

"Please show me, Lord. What attitude should I take toward this woman?" she prayed.

The answer came—a word from heaven. Forgive. ". . . if any man have a quarrel against any: even as Christ forgave you, so also do ye" (Colossians 3:13).

Forgive? Was that it?

Mabel decided, God helping her, she could do

that. And she did. She let go of wanting to have the last word in the awful matter, of wanting to fight back and somehow punish this woman for what she had done.

Immediately everything changed. As far as Mabel was concerned, it was as though the whole thing had never happened. All the bad feelings that had been plaguing her were simply gone.

And she did not get called back to the States.

Not every manifestation of self is meanness and ugliness, Mabel learned. Self can be found to be behind even good deeds. Being "nice" has its rewards. Like having others notice how nice you are and remarking about it. Then self is filled with pride and revels in the glory of being such a good person.

While singing a hymn with a group of Japanese young people, Mabel became convicted of the problem that this "nice" self can be, and how firmly entrenched it was in her life.

> Make me a captive, Lord.
> And then I shall be free;
> Force me to render up my sword,
> And I shall conqueror be.

So went the words by George Matheson. The line about rendering up one's sword suddenly over-whelmed Mabel, and she had to go into another room and kneel before the Lord. Yes, she had a sword that needed to be surrendered—a sword that was always at the ready to slash away any suggestion that Mabel Francis was at fault.

It was taking a long time, but Mabel was learning that everything God allowed to come into her life had a purpose. If He allowed someone to be rude to her, the issue was not the person who caused the trouble but how she would react. She came to realize that no matter how painful the lesson, it shed some new light on the self problem, and she could only say, "O Lord, I am thankful to You for showing me this."

She was learning that God did not want her to be *struggling* to be like Christ, *trying* to be good. What He wanted her to do was to let the only Good One come and take over. This was her inheritance in Christ. This was why Jesus died on the cross.

If a rich relative left her a million dollars, would she settle for five hundred? No! She would want the whole inheritance, not just part of it. A change of attitude was called for. In order for that to happen in her spiritual life, the old self had to go. Now she was beginning to understand about being crucified with Christ . . . dying to self . . . denying self. It was "not I, but Christ," just as Galatians 2:20 said. Or in the words of John the Baptist, "I must decrease, He must increase" (John 3:30).

In the fall, feeling the need to be alone and rest for a few days, Mabel went up to a resort in the mountains where people went to escape the heat of the lowlands. The summer people having gone, by now, she felt as if she had the whole mountain to herself.

Except for God . . . and the enemy.

Satan tormented her with the thought that she would never survive this time of testing that she had been going through. She would go back to the States a nervous wreck, and that would be the end of her.

It was not difficult to believe that could happen. Even now she was not well. If she hadn't had a nervous breakdown, she had come close. But she would not listen to Satan's taunts. From the top of the mountain she cried out, "I will not doubt. All you demons in hell, listen! I will not doubt! My God will make Himself known to the Japanese people through me!"

A wonderful revelation came to Mabel during this time of soul searching and seeking God. "The Lord thy God in the midst of thee is mighty," Zephaniah 3:17 said. It was a Scripture verse she had known for many years. Yes, God was in the midst of His people *and* He was "in the midst" of Mabel Francis.

She had reached a milestone; she was filled with a new realization of the presence of Christ within her. His resurrection life flowed through every nerve of her body, every organ, bringing healing and strength and peace. Jesus had taken over. He was now Lord and King! It was just as Dr. Simpson had written:

> The crisis has been passed,
> And I have come at last
> Into the promised land of peace and rest.
> The crisis hour is o'er,
> And now forevermore
> I am dwelling in God's blessing and God's best.
>
> It came, I know not how,
> But this I know, that now
> My life has found a new and nobler plane.

Something has passed away,
Something has come to stay,
And I can never be the same again.

The change is not in me;
Rather it seems that He
Has come Himself to live His life in mine;
And as I stepped aside
And took Him to abide,
He came and filled me with His life divine.

Though troubles still came, the fretting and irritation were gone. She was free! And she was so perfectly healed that she scarcely realized she had a nerve in her body.

Back in America on furlough, Mabel was one of the featured speakers at a Christian and Misssionary Alliance camp in Keswick, Canada. Her nieces, Ida and Gladys Francis, who lived in New Jersey, accompanied her to Canada and to some of her other speaking engagements, and she spent some time in their home. This was a different Aunt Mabel, the nieces were to remark later. When they were children, they had been a bit uncomfortable with their Aunt Mabel because she was inclined to pressure them about being better Christians. Now a compelling inner beauty and joy drew them to her and to her Lord.

8

War Clouds

WAR CLOUDS had been hovering over Japan for some time. The Japanese military, having won victories over China and Korea, were now chafing to teach a lesson to the United States, which they felt had affronted them. The troubles began with immigration problems between the two countries. Then it was one thing after another added to already strained relations.

No one had to tell Mabel that there were problems between the two countries. She could feel the animosity and suspicion. And one day a policeman was posted outside her house to keep daily track of her.

"War with the United States will break out very soon," he confided one day.

"Oh, no!" Mabel responded. "Don't let them do it! You have no idea how big and strong America is."

"I know," he answered, "but I think we can do it."

Somehow, the Japanese military clique was able to sweep even the Emperor himself along with the idea that war was inevitable: Japan was being surrounded by the "ABCD encirclement"—the Americans, the British, the Chinese and the Dutch, they told him. If the Japanese did not strike very soon, the other nations would, and Japan would be destroyed. The Emperor's personal newspaper gave him only what they wanted him to know, with some clever manipulation thrown in besides.

As an American standing on the sidelines watching what was going on in Japan, Mabel could easily see the great difference between American and Japanese thinking. During her years in Japan she had seen many occasions for grief and suffering—fires, floods, disease, the great earthquake in 1923. To the Japanese mind, these were all worse than war. According to Japanese beliefs, those who died fighting for the Emperor would immediately enter into an eternal paradise of bliss. What happened to the souls of those who died in other disasters, no one knew. The hopelessness could be seen in the crowds that thronged the wooden shrines where the bones of such victims reposed.

More and more Mabel felt that being out among the Japanese was only stirring up animosity. Instead, her work became that of ministering to the Japanese who came to her. The house in Matsuyama became a little hospital where several Japanese who had nowhere else to go were cared for.

One of Mabel's patients was a government official's wife with tuberculosis. Another was a young man who had been in the Bible school, and he, too, had tuberculosis. His own family was afraid of the disease and didn't want him to come home. The ill wife of one of the Japanese pastors also found refuge in the little hospital.

Mabel's brother Tom was becoming more and more troubled by the suspicion and animosity he was encountering. Engaged in a successful ministry throughout the area starting new churches, he did a great deal of traveling and visiting with the Japanese. Because he was a big man, he found the Japanese custom of sitting on the floor quite uncomfortable, so he made a box to sit on when he was visiting in Japanese homes. This he strapped on the back of his bicycle, and carried his Bible and other teaching materials in it from place to place. To the Japanese, this box—it was painted black—looked suspicious. Surely it had some anti-Japanese purpose. He would often be stopped by a policeman or government agent asking, "What do you have in that box?" And Tom, bristling with indignation, would have to open the box for inspection.

Finally, he became so frustrated with such interference in his work that he returned to the States, hoping everything would blow over shortly.

Anne and Mabel in the meantime were keeping in touch by mail. Anne was working in Fukuyama on Honshu Island on the other side of the Inland Sea from Matsuyama, located on Shikoku. Though their letters were censored they conferred as to what they should do, if matters became worse. Should they, too, return to the States as they had been advised by friends, and even the American Consul? What would happen if they stayed in Japan?

It was not as though they were tourists. Mabel had been in Japan by this time for over thirty years, and Anne for well over ten. But more than that, they had come to Japan by the command of God Himself. They couldn't just pick up and leave without word from Him.

The answer came from two portions of Scripture. One, for their missionary work, was a promise from Isaiah 45:3: "I will give thee the treasures of darkness and the hidden riches of secret places." For their own strength and assurance was the thought from Deuteronomy 32:30 of one chasing a thousand, and two putting ten thousand to flight. That was good enough for Anne and Mabel. They would stay in Japan.

Secretly, Japan began to fortify the most important of her island possessions, and built more and bigger ships. By 1940 Japan was warring in China, and finally accomplished the military occupation of French Indochina.

In August 1941, the United States warned that further aggression would be met by the United States with whatever steps might be necessary to put a halt to it. President Roosevelt ordered a stop to all American trade with Japan, cutting off most of the oil and steel necessary for war industries.

In October the new prime minister, General Hideki Tojo, began plans for an early war against the United States. Japan's fighting forces were large, efficient, and ready for war.

The situation was looking more and more

perilous. Mabel and Anne decided that in order not to be hampered by possessions, should the worst happen they would bury their personal belongings—family keepsakes and the like—in the yard at Hiroshima for safekeeping until the war was over. However, they were perfectly at peace about their decision to stay in Japan, come what may. They had heard the sweet, still small voice of the Spirit of God assuring them of His protection. "War cannot break out until I permit it," He told them, "and when I do permit it, I will take care of you. There is no need to fear."

This was familiar ground. The Lord had faithfully led them when the mission had pulled out of Japan a few years earlier. He hadn't failed then, and He wouldn't fail now.

Mabel longed to be able to see Anne face to face, but the authorities would not allow either of them to cross the Inland Sea.

One day, as she was praying, she had a vision of two men, each holding back a dog on a leash, the dogs struggling to get at each other. Again the Lord reassured her, "I hold this whole situation. It won't break until I get ready for it to break. I hold both sides, so you don't need to worry. When I let it come, I'll have you on My mind. I will take care of you."

9

The War

"SENSEI! It's come, it's come!" Akiko, one of the girls who worked for Mabel, cried as she burst into the house that December morning in 1941.

Mabel ran to see what all the fuss was about.

"The war, Sensei, the war! It has broken out," Akiko shouted.

"Oh, it can't be!" Mabel said.

"Yes, it is true, it has broken out!" Akiko was almost screaming now.

But, of course, there was nothing to be done about it. Just wait and see what would happen.

The next day the police came to Mabel's house. "Do you realize that you are now classified as an enemy national?" one of them asked.

"Yes," Mabel answered, but assured them that she had no intention of doing anything harmful. "I am still a guest in Japan."

There were papers to sign indicating her enemy national status. For the time being, however, she would be allowed to stay in her own house. The only requirement was that she keep a record in a little black book the police left with her of all visitors and of her own activities. Fair enough under the circumstances, Mabel felt.

Anne, across the Inland Sea in Fukuyama, did not get off so easily. Just three hours after the declaration of war was broadcast, the police arrived at her home. Allowing her only a few minutes to pack essentials, they marched her off to the police station. Here she spent three days . . . praying and wondering if Mabel was going through the same experience. The Fukuyama jail turned out to be only a stopover. Her destination was the mountain prison camp at Miyoshi.

Word of her transfer spread quickly to all of the churches. As she was taken under guard to the camp by train, groups of believers boarded the train, each at their own station, and rode to the next station, hoping to give a little comfort by their presence along the way.

Ordinarily, under such circumstances, a basket would have been put over the head of the prisoner. The police proved their kindness by not following this custom, so Anne was able to see those who cared so deeply for her even though she was not permitted to speak with them.

At Miyoshi, an Englishman, two English teachers, a drug addict, a priest and eleven nuns became her companions. Though communicating with anyone outside the camp was against the rules, the officer in charge of the camp permitted Anne to write to Mabel and personally mailed her letters. Not only that, but he allowed Anne to receive Mabel's letters, and he informed Mabel that she would be allowed to send food to Anne.

As for Mabel back in Matsuyama, things continued pretty much the same for some time. For the present, the main concern of the police there seemed to be enforcing complete loyalty to the government.

One of the policemen assigned to keep tabs on the activities of the American missionary decided to take advantage of the situation to advance himself. He told the authorities that Pastor Ogata was telling Mabel things about the war that were not suitable for her as an enemy alien to know.

The other policeman, the senior officer, sensed that Mabel was troubled and questioned her about it.

"Well, I'll just take care of that," he said when he understood the situation. And he did. Whether the other policeman ever got a promotion, Mabel never found out, but at least he didn't get one at Pastor Ogata's expense.

Akiko stayed on with Mabel, proving herself a loving, devoted companion, although she was suspect because of her association with the American missionary and was warned to leave. She brought in many of the daily needs of food. Another friend, a teacher, sent in garden produce and chickens regularly, as well as *mai sau*, fermented beans for soup, which provided real nourishment when other food was scarce.

Mabel was deeply touched by the kindness and concern of her Japanese friends during this period. How attitudes had changed since her early days in Japan!

Almost a year had gone by when one day three policemen came to Mabel's door. She was informed that tomorrow she would be taking the train to Yokohama. What was to become of her at Yokohama they didn't say.

"But what about the sick people in my house?" Mabel inquired.

"We'll take care of them," she was assured. "They will go to the hospital if necessary."

There was nothing to do but accept the inevitable, for it seemed that the Holy Spirit said to her, "Don't say a word. You must do as you are told."

Mabel's Christian friends and neighbors prepared a farewell meal. As she described the get-together later, it was a blessed time in spite of the going-away feeling. She gave away most of her belongings to those who had come to say goodbye.

And then it was tomorrow. But what of Anne?

"I am not going without some word from my sister," Mabel told the police.

"She will be with you," they assured her without hesitation.

Because it was a disgrace to be seen walking with a policeman, Mabel's escort to the train station kindly walked ahead, allowing her to follow him.

All of Mabel's Japanese friends felt sorry about what was happening, though they wouldn't have dared make a public demonstration. Now as she made her way along the street behind the policeman, some watched, unable to stop the flowing tears. Others, with no sign of outward emotion, signaled almost imperceptibly with a flutter of their fingers, adding their own farewell.

Mabel was overwhelmed by this show of respect and friendship and regard at this time when she was a prisoner and an enemy national. It meant even more in view of the fact that now the emotions of the people were manipulated by propagandists until they didn't know what to believe.

The pastor in Matsuyama and some of the other believers were given permission to accompany Mabel on the train. Under other circumstances it would have been a pleasant journey. No one would have known that here was a prisoner under police guard.

Upon arrival in Yokohama, Mabel soon realized that she was indeed a prisoner. And she was one of a group of Americans who were to be exchanged for Japanese prisoners in the United States.

But what of her decision to stay in Japan? She had been so sure that it had been God's will that she stay. However, there was nothing to be done about it. If the Japanese government deported her, she was deported, and that was that.

From the window of the room she was assigned, she could see ships in the harbor. One had large white crosses painted on its side.

Nothing happened for several days; then from her window, Mabel saw workmen painting over the white crosses. The exchange was off, she learned. The Japanese had wanted to send all the Americans back to their own country. When the American officials learned that those being sent were staying in Japan by their own decision, they refused to go along with the exchange.

Now what? And where was Anne?

Soon two paddy wagons, or Black Marias, arrived at the hotel where the American deportees were quartered, and they were herded into them. The destination was a hotel in Tokyo where they stayed for a short time before being transferred to a large house that had been part of a Catholic orphanage. Here they were examined and questioned like true enemy aliens, and assigned rooms.

Now, how to get her belongings to her room? Everything was in her trunk and it was too heavy for her to carry.

"Who can I get to help me with my trunk?" Mabel asked the policeman guard.

With a sneer, he replied, "Who do you think you are? You are just an enemy national—carry your own trunk!"

The words cut like a knife. After all the years of service and ministry to the Japanese, was this all the appreciation she would get? "No matter!" the Holy Spirit reminded her. Had she come to Japan to be appreciated?

"Dear Lord, forgive me!" Mabel whispered. "I really have not come here to be appreciated. I have come here to witness to your love!"

As for the trunk, with the help of some of Mabel's fellow internees it found its way to her room.

Some weeks passed with no word from Anne until late one day, as Mabel was looking out a window, she saw a group of prisoners arrive and who should be among them but Anne herself!

And then they were face to face! "Oh, Andy!" Mabel cried out, the girlhood name rushing to her lips in joy.

Seeking an escape from the confusion of the newly arrived group, Mabel guided her sister to a back stairway where they could revel in private over the wonder of being together again. Was it really happening?

Even when Mabel had first seen Anne arriving with the other prisoners from Miyoshi, she sensed that the past year had been an ordeal for her sister. And the trials were not to end now that they were together.

First of all, conditions were crowded. There were well over 150 women internees, some ninety Catholic nuns and the rest Protestant missionaries and teachers. The only place left for Anne to sleep was on the floor in front of the doorway. Anybody coming and going had to step over her head. Still, it was a great comfort to be together again. Now they were able to share, to pray and study together. The Lord had brought them together to encourage each other in the hard times that lay ahead.

There was one final opportunity to return to America on the Swedish steamship *Gripsholm*.

"We think you had better go," the police advised the internees. "We can't promise what may happen."

Most of the Catholic nuns, as well as quite a few of the Protestant women, decided to take advantage of this opportunity, but Anne and Mabel, along with a number of the others, stuck with their initial decision. They felt certain that it was the will of God for them to stay.

It was a lonely feeling seeing so many of their compatriots leave, knowing that with the sailing of the *Gripsholm* this was absolutely the last chance. They were in Japan as enemy aliens for the duration, for better or for worse. Nevertheless, they felt great peace in their committment to what they felt God wanted them to do. They could trust Him to take care of them.

Conditions were quite tolerable at first. A Swiss monk was in charge of the welfare of the prisoners. They had their own cook, and food was adequate. Occasionally the monk would bring some jam or other little treat from the American Embassy.

They were allowed to read and study among themselves. Books which probably had belonged to the American ambassador were brought over from the Embassy. Mabel read American history, including a biography of Abraham Lincoln. And because it seemed to her that it would be good to try something new and challenging, she began to learn French under the teaching of the French nuns. Having time on her hands to read and study was a new experience after the years of missionary activity. The outside world and those days seemed far removed from life now in this quiet place.

One disturber of the peace was a loud, ill-tempered fellow who served as an errand boy for the police. Anne was afraid of him, he was so unpredictable. The slightest provocation could cause him to fly off into a rage at any time.

One morning one of the nuns had gotten a tub of warm water to do some laundry. Water hot enough for washing clothes was hard to come by. Then along came the troublemaker. He wanted the tub to do some laundry of his own and said so in his rude way.

The saintly sister offered to do his laundry for him when she had finished.

But no, he would do it himself, and he would do it now. He dumped out the nun's laundry, warm water and all, and went off with the tub.

As months passed, the food became worse and worse. It had been the understanding of the prisoners that the Japanese government had made provision for food for their class of prisoners. Why was there so little food, and why was it so bad?

Soy beans were sometimes on the menu, but apparently the cook did not realize—or perhaps he didn't care—that soy beans need to be cooked and cooked and cooked before they are edible. Mercifully, the beans were sometimes ground and made into a soup which went down all right.

Acccording to international law an internee must be given one pound of bread each day. Two small buns make a pound. At first the bread was all right, but it became worse and worse because of a lack of flour. Finally the day came when the bread was made of peanut shucks and corn cobs ground up fine. Two of those buns made breakfast. At noon there was a cup of watered-down rice. That came to be the food ration for the day as time progressed. If you wanted something to eat in the evening so as not to be too hungry to sleep, you had to save some of the noon's rice ration.

"Give us this day our daily bread" was not just a prayer one recited without thinking. These prisoners prayed it with their whole hearts.

Mabel would never forget the day that the guard told them, "No bread today—we just don't have any!"

"All right, Lord," the prisoners prayed, "if You want us to go without bread today, it is all right with us."

That very day, though, a Japanese neighbor arrived with a big basket of spinach sprouts she had dug from her garden to make room to plant something else.

So they had spinach. And wasn't it good!

The day never came, as nearly as Mabel can remember, that there was absolutely nothing to eat. It might not have been what they would have liked, but there was something! They learned to eat things they wouldn't ordinarily have eaten—like stems and sprouts of sweet potatoes. Or orange peels—put them in buns and make believe you have bread and jam!

Salt was something that was sometimes missing. Sugar is much easier to get along without than salt. On one occasion, the only salt they had was a dirty chunk of hard salt of the kind put out for cattle to lick. But no matter. It was salt!

A true godsend were the boxes of food sent in by the International Red Cross on three occasions. These contained corned beef, powdered milk, sugar, raisins and a can of fruit. Mabel found that having these occasional treats made it easier to accept the usual bad camp fare.

After some time they discovered that the cook was selling much of the food and pocketing the profits. After all, what did it matter about the welfare of enemy alien prisoners? Nothing, apparently, to this man.

On the other hand, the man in charge of the camp was a good and considerate man as far as it was within his power, though he was sometimes curt and brusque.

The internees were allowed to have some money, but they could not go out to spend it. On occasion they would give money to the camp supervisor and he himself would go out and buy what they needed.

After the war he became a Christian and served as a deacon in one of the Protestant congregations in Tokyo. "I saw that you people had something that I didn't know anything about," he told Mabel. That something was the love of Christ that made it possible to love one's enemies.

By the summer of 1945 the world outside was becoming more and more a part of life for those inside the prison camp. Though they were not told what was going on as far as the war was concerned, the prisoners could hear the American B-29s overhead every night, and bombs exploding. Fires raged all around. More than half the city of Tokyo lay in ruins.

Nightly now the prisoners were herded into the basement as sirens signaled that American bombers were approaching.

"Mabel," Anne whispered one night as the explosions came closer and yet closer, "if they would make just one second's mistake in letting those bombs go, they would fall right on us."

That was one thing they didn't need to be afraid of, Mabel assured her sister. "We have been here all this time at God's command, and with His promise that one shall chase a thousand and two put ten thousand to flight, it just wouldn't read right that we stayed in Japan at God's command only to be killed by mistake in an American bombing raid."

Though drained and weary after four years of internment and well aware of the danger of their position, Mabel, now sixty-five years of age, was occupied with thoughts of the great spiritual and emotional needs of the Japanese when defeat came. Surely it was only a matter of time. Even among the Japanese there was a sense of impending doom, though none dared express it aloud.

Finally word came that the Emperor's palace had been bombed and burned. As far as the safety of the prison camp, the officials thought it relatively safe because it was some distance from other buildings. But one night soon after the bombing of the Emperor's palace, nearby Waseda University was hit, and as that burned, the flames blew over into the prison building.

Word came to evacuate: Hurry down the steps, out the back door, and wait together at a certain place on the next street. The women didn't need to be told twice.

There on the street they numbly watched the last of their belongings going up in flames.

When the prison officials appeared, it was apparent that there was no plan set up for such an emergency as this.

"Just start walking," the women were told.

They walked and walked until daylight. On that desolate walk through the bombed and burning streets they saw many heartbreaking sights, like the mother with whimpering children clinging to her, her husband killed, their home destroyed. Where could they go? What could they do?

The prisoners with their guards had no answer.

At last they arrived at an abandoned school building. From somewhere hardtack and water appeared, which was most welcome. Mabel wanted desperately to wash her face and tried to do so in a fish bowl.

A man came up to her. "Come over here, lady, and I will show you a place to wash."

Mabel followed him to a little pond in his yard just outside the gate. As soon as the guards saw where she had gone, they came running after her shouting, "Don't you know she can't go out?" And they pulled her back inside the fence. But she had gotten her face washed anyway.

The prisoners spent the night in a Franciscan hospital, all in one room that was also overpopulated with mosquitoes. And no mosquito nets. A good combination for a miserable night.

On the sixth of August the atomic bomb was dropped on the city of Hiroshima. Three days later a second bomb destroyed Nagasaki. However, the prisoners and even the Japanese around them, if they knew of the bombings, had no realization of the indescribable destruction the bombing had brought.

Even without this added incentive, the Japanese, except for a few of the military and government leaders, were ready to surrender.

All through the war the Emperor's military and government advisors had managed to deceive him as to what was actually the truth in regard to the war. In the newspaper that was prepared especially for him, he had been given only what information they wanted him to have. When the imperial palace was bombed, however, he finally realized what had been happening. The report that he received said that the palace was only slightly damaged.

"Slightly damaged!" he exclaimed. "Why, it is completely gone!"

It was announced that on the fifteenth day of August a momentous thing would happen. The Emperor himself would speak on the radio.

When that day arrived, the people were shaking and choked with emotion. Never before had they heard the voice of him whom they considered to be a god. What would he say? Many had the idea that he would command all of the Japanese to commit suicide rather than fall into enemy hands.

Mabel and Anne listened to the radio that morning with the nurses and others in the hospital where they were being quartered.

The Emperor, close to weeping, spoke with tenderness as he announced that the war was over. The people of Japan had endured enough suffering, he declared. "We are keenly aware of you, our subjects. However, it is according to the dictate of time and fate that we have resolved to pave the way for a grand peace for all generations to come by enduring the unendurable and suffering the insufferable."

The war was over! Some of the leaders who disagreed with the Emperor committed suicide. Some people dropped dead at the shock of it all. Some just fell into an exhausted sleep right on the street. Anne and Mabel and their companions were told to go back to their rooms. They would be informed later about their release.

Two weeks later they were still in the internment camp. There was nowhere to go in war-battered Tokyo. There were no vehicles for transportation, and not even communication with the outside.

American planes began to drop provisions for those in need, though the parachutes were not made for dropping parcels. Many of the cases of food were broken upon impact with the ground. In one case of canned fruit, every can had been broken open, spilling out all the juice. Juice or not, the fruit was welcome and the Americans shared it with the people in the hospital, along with sugar and other items.

Cases of men's clothing were also dropped, probably with GI prisoners of war in mind. The Japanese camp leader helped distribute the clothing, and selected a suit for himself. Dressed in his new finery, he came around to the prisoners' rooms and, saluting them, said, "My dear ladies, you are now free!"

10

Afterward: Tokyo

CHAOS and despair ruled everywhere in war-torn Tokyo. Everything was in ruins. Going anywhere in the city involved finding a way around ruined buildings, piles of rubble, abandoned trucks and vehicles that had been bombed and burned. The only transportation available was by train, and that was an ordeal in itself. Besides being old and worn out, the trains were crowded beyond belief. The aisles were so full that when people couldn't get in through the doors, they would come in through the windows and onto the laps of those who had been fortunate enough to find seats.

The American occupation army headed by General Douglas MacArthur arrived and began to bring order to the chaos.

"Let's get the missionaries back in Japan," General MacArthur said. "There is a vacuum here that only the missionaries can fill."

But unbeknown to the General, two missionaries, Mabel Francis and her sister Anne Dievendorf, were already there, bright-faced, smiling and eager to get to work: Two little old ladies, all alone, no mission board behind them. No one to appeal to but God.

They claimed the promise of Second Chronicles 16:9: "The eyes of the Lord run to and fro throughout the whole earth to show himself strong in the behalf of them whose heart is perfect toward him."

Yes, the Lord would show Himself strong! Let the miracles begin!

A group of soldiers with the American forces spotted Anne one day on a crowded Tokyo train. "She's got to be an American missionary!" one young man declared when he saw her smile. Just what they were looking for!

The soldiers followed her when she made her way out of the train.

"We didn't know where to get hold of an American missionary, but we are looking for a place where we can meet and go on with our gospel hour which we started in the Philippines," they told her when they had caught up with her.

She took the men to the Japanese pastor of the First Methodist Church, right on the Ginza, the main street of Tokyo. The pastor was delighted at the idea of having these Christian Americans use the church. There was a big hole that a bomb had left in the roof, but no matter! Soon joyful songs of praise to God were sounding out night after night all over the center of war-sick Tokyo through that hole in the roof.

There came to be perhaps 400 young men involved in these gospel services as time went on.

When the Japanese found out that they, too, were welcome, they crowded in until they nearly crowded out the GIs. Though many could not understand English, they understood the joy and earnestness in the faces of the American soldiers. When an invitation was given, they came forward eager for whatever it was that these Americans had.

The GIs had gotten Japanese Testaments and marked the passages which they could point out to the seekers. Many of them learned to read some of these passages in Japanese.

Only God knows the thousands of Japanese people who were affected by these American soldiers who sang and preached and prayed and helped during every spare moment away from their duties with the occupation forces.

At the center of all this—interpreting, guiding, assisting, calling, distributing clothing and food to the needy of Tokyo—were the bright, happy American missionary ladies. God had given them their immediate ministry in Tokyo.

Anne and Mabel were concerned about the Christians who might still be alive at Matsuyama, Hiroshima, Fukuyama and other cities where there had been churches before the war. For now, travel to those cities was impossible. There was not even any way to communicate with them.

In those tension-filled days the American soldiers, particularly the Christians, seemed heaven-sent, even to the Japanese. How different from what they had expected! Although there were exceptions, many were the accounts of the kindness of the Americans and their willingness to help the Japanese.

"We thought that when these American soldiers came in that all of the women would be molested and that we would have a terrible time," one woman said. "So in our neighborhood we strung up a system of bells, and if anyone was molested, she would ring the bells and we would all come and get him—we would kill him!

"But we didn't need to feel like that," she continued. "They have been so kind." She related an incident in which an American soldier had seen to it that she was given a seat on the tram when she was carrying a heavy load.

The American chaplains would personally see to it that food that might have been thrown away because of army regulations found its way to the hungry Japanese.

Even General MacArthur made himself available to help the Japanese. He was a champion of the women, accustomed to being considered second-class citizens. He listened to their needs and gave them the right to vote.

"If only there could have been more missionaries to lead the Japanese in the right direction," Mabel was to lament in years to come. General MacArthur asked for a thousand missionaries. They never came!

11

Matsuyama:
Beginning Again

WINTER arrived and Anne and Mabel were still in Tokyo. Not until February of 1946 were they able to get to Matsuyama.

The destruction in Matsuyama was even worse than in Tokyo. All the churches had been destroyed. Everything was gone! Only one house remained standing in the entire neighborhood where Mabel had lived.

How did it happen that that one house had survived? they wondered.

As soon as they went inside they understood.

In hopes of lessening damage during the bombings, most people had pasted strips of heavy paper over the seams and windows of their houses. The lady of this particular house had decided that the strips of paper she used should mean something. "The battle is not yours, but God's," was written on one strip. On another, "Ye shall not need to fight in this battle," and another, "The Lord your God, He it is that fighteth for you."

An upstairs room in this very house became home

to the two American missionaries. It was a small room, only eight by twelve feet—space enough for a bed, but that was about all. Except for sleeping, all living was done Japanese style—on the floor.

Now, having found a place to live, they would have to figure out some way to get the missionary work started again. But how and where? They would need a building of some sort, but there simply was no material for building anything.

Mabel remembered reading of a doctor in China who had "prayed up" the walls of a hospital. Well, if he could pray up the walls of a hospital, they could certainly pray up the walls of a church. So they began to pray.

Meanwhile, they were able to find the man who had been the pastor of the church in Matsuyama, along with a few of the members. And during their search they heard some promising news: One of the American contingency military units would be moving out soon. Some things probably would be thrown away during the move. Anne and Mabel decided to call on the officer in charge, just in case. They would be glad for just about anything, even an old chair.

Upon arrival at the base they found that it was the military police unit that was moving out. Not likely that they would have anything. Well, it wouldn't hurt to check it out, anyway, since they were there.

They timidly knocked on the door of the outer office. A big, burly, blue-eyed Irishman came to the door.

He looked his visitors over from head to foot.

"Well, girls, where did you come from?" he asked, and invited them in.

They explained where they had come from and why they were there. "We would be glad for even a board," they told him.

He thought for a few moments and then told them about a house on the airfield that the army had condemned. It was scheduled to be pulled off into the sea. "There's a lot of good material in that house. Would you like to go down and take a look at it?"

Gladly they piled into a jeep with the officer and his driver, and off they went. On the way they were stopped by another jeep that pulled right in front of them, blocking their way. Officers with angry faces jumped out ready to confront the driver. Didn't he know it was absolutely against the rules for an American to transport ladies?

And then they got a good look at the ladies that were being transported. These were not the kind of ladies they had expected to see!

"Where did you get them?" the men asked, utterly flabbergasted.

When their story was told, Anne and Mabel and their escort were allowed to drive on.

The possibilities of the building were far beyond the missionaries' expectation. It was made of corrugated iron, and there was even electrical wiring, which couldn't have been bought anywhere in Japan at that time. An added bonus was a big table of thick plywood, also unobtainable in Japan. Could they use the building? Yes! Practically everything!

"Just one stipulation," the colonel said. "Everything has to be off the base in three days—that's our deadline for having everything cleared up when we leave."

Three days! Anne and Mabel looked at each other. They didn't even have a hammer!

"We'll loan you hammers," the Colonel offered.

So Anne and Mabel suddenly found themselves in the demolition business. With the help of a Japanese boy, they set to work with heavy claw hammers, loosening great strips of corrugated iron and laying them together in piles on the ground.

Every once in a while the two sisters would look at each other and say, "How are we ever going to carry all this into the city?" There were no trucks to be hired, that was certain.

They turned back to their work with a prayer, "Lord, you know all about this. You know this material has to be carried up to the city somehow."

Toward evening a big American army truck pulled up to the site. The colonel was worrying about how they were going to get the materials from the base into the city and had sent the truck to help.

By then the demolition crew of three had gotten the corrugated sheets off the lower part of the building, but there was still work to be done higher up. The truck driver, seeing the situation, hitched the truck onto one corner of the remaining framework and down it all came at once. Now finishing the job would be much easier.

Then along came some soldiers who loaded the

salvaged material onto the truck. Anne and Mabel and their helper couldn't have been happier. There was no way they could have done it all themselves.

Well ahead of deadline, the building was removed from the Army base and the materials deposited on the property in Matsuyama where it would be used to build a church.

This was only the beginning of miracles in connection with rebuilding the mission work.

The missionaries learned of another group of Army base buildings that was to be disposed of. They went immediately to check it out. This colonel, however, was not as sympathetic as the first one. Americans were not in Japan to build churches, he told them. And that was that!

The Japanese man who had told them of the disposal urged them to try once more.

Reluctantly Anne and Mabel went back to the base. The colonel had just been transferred, they were told, and were referred to his successor.

"Of course, you ought to have one of those buildings," the new colonel said without hesitation. However, this time there was some government red tape that had to be taken care of. A properly written petition would have to be presented to the governor of the precinct.

That sounded pretty complicated to Anne and Mabel. Maybe they had better forget this idea. But their Japanese friend urged them not to give up and took it upon himself to write the petition.

When they presented it to the governor, he called

for his aide who was in charge of such matters. When the aide appeared, who should it be but the very man who had prepared the petition. Not surprisingly, he assured the governor that the document was in proper order and concurred in the opinion that the missionaries should have one of the buildings.

From these two buildings came adequate material to build the church they had in mind, with enough left over for a smaller one. All at a time when it was impossible to buy anything.

Besides building materials, the second colonel gave the missionaries the food that the transferred unit couldn't take with them. Included in this windfall were several cases of eggs (ten dozen eggs in a case) and—luxury of luxuries!—several great chunks of link sausage, which Anne and Mabel and their Japanese friends enjoyed for many days.

What joy the missionary sisters had in sharing this bounty! And what an encouragement it was to be able to help the Japanese. Here was more evidence that they hadn't stayed in Japan in vain.

For a time, Mabel served as liaison between the occupation army and the Japanese government by directing the distribution of relief goods to destitute families.

Soon the new church building in Matsuyama began to take shape, but with the limited funds on hand it would be a while before it was finished.

"Let's go back up to Tokyo," Mabel suggested to Anne. "I think we ought to have an audience with General MacArthur and see if he won't make a way for us to get some funds."

Anne agreed. There was no question but that they needed money. Probably brother Tom would have some available in the States, but at this point they would need the General's influence to get it. They did not know then that Tom had died of a heart attack during the war.

When Anne and Mabel got to Tokyo, whom should they meet but one of the young Christian soldiers with whom they had worked immediately after the surrender.

"Tell me all about your work and how things are going down in Matsuyama," he said, and then changed his mind. "No, don't tell me now. Come to the meeting tonight so that all of the boys will have a chance to hear."

Anne and Mabel accepted the invitation and renewed acquaintance with their friends in the bombed-out church in downtown Tokyo.

When they had finished telling their story, one of the young men stood up and said to the others, "Say, we want to have a part in this, don't we?"

Of course they did, his fellow servicemen agreed. They took up a spur-of-the-moment collection which amounted to the incredible sum of 200,000 Japanese yen, equal to about $550.

Anne and Mabel went back to Matsuyama without having an audience with General MacArthur after all. And the church building in Matsuyama was finished debt free!

12

Hiroshima: Beginning Again

HIROSHIMA had been a great and beautiful city. For Mabel, it had been the center of her missionary work before the war. The Bible school had been in Hiroshima. Now the city was a desolate wilderness.

Few people realized the terrible destruction wrought by the atomic bomb when it was dropped on Hiroshima. In the internment camp the prisoners had been told that a terrible new weapon had been used against the Japanese, but just how terrible could not be imagined by anyone who had not been there when it happened.

The bomb came suddenly in a blast of fiery light. There was no escape. Those in the center of the blast just disintegrated with no trace left of them. Stones fused together under that light. The concussion from the blast was so strong that people's eyes were pulled out of their heads. Many other people saw their loved ones burned alive. The river was jammed with the dead bodies of those who had rushed there in desperation, seeking relief from the terrible pain.

When Mabel first returned to Hiroshima, she couldn't find anyone she knew. She intended to do something about beginning the work again, but she could find no place to stay. A Japanese soldier she met told her that though he had been searching the area for three weeks, he could find no trace of his family. A Japanese lady who had been out of town the morning of the blast was never able to find any of her family, either.

Not until her third trip to Hiroshima did Mabel finally find one of the men from the Hiroshima church. He was putting up a shack on the main street in order to get his business going again.

He had only a little shelter for his family. It was so small that when everybody was laid out at night the floor was covered. Nevertheless, he and his wife invited Mabel to stay with them, because they were so eager to help get the church going again in Hiroshima. To make room, they sent the children to relatives in the country.

The day after arriving in Hiroshima for the third time, Mabel found a piece of property suitable for building a church. She also located Kuniji Oye who had been an outstanding leader in the church before the war.

Mabel told him about the property. The problem was, she couldn't oversee building a church in Hiroshima and still live in Matsuyama. And of course she couldn't stay indefinitely in the little shelter over on Main Street.

"Let's take the whole matter to God," he advised.

So they asked the Lord to send someone to oversee the building and to pastor the church.

The person God sent was Mr. Oye's son, Suteichi Oye, a pastor himself, who would someday become the president of the national church in Japan. During the war the younger Mr. Oye had been imprisoned because of his faith and his strong stand against the war and the military forces.

Weak and in poor health after his release, he had turned to business, but could not get away from the call to preach the gospel. He came to talk to Mabel and others of the church about the possibility of ministering in Hiroshima.

"I know of your work and your faith," Mabel told him. "I would very much like to have you join us and take up the work in Hiroshima. But I can't offer you a salary, for I don't have one myself. I trust God for my living from day to day."

Mr. Oye decided he would come. If Mabel could trust God, he could too!

But where would he and his family live? The church now owned a piece of land, but there were no buildings on it.

The problem was solved when Mr. Oye's uncle, an American citizen who had been stranded in Japan during the war, suddenly received a visa so he could return to America. He had gathered materials to build himself a small two-room building. He was happy to give the materials to his nephew. They could be used to build a little shack to live in while the church was being built.

A permit from the city had to be issued to build the church. The officials to whom they presented their plans were both puzzled and intrigued with the size of the church they were planning.

"Why such a big church?"

Simply because they would need plenty of room.

"How much money do you have for the project?"

"Well, no money," Mabel admitted. But they had faith in the living God.

The officials looked as though they thought this American missionary lady was out of her mind. Mr. Oye, who had come along with Mabel, could understand how they felt.

In spite of what they must have thought, for some reason permission was granted to build the church.

They found a carpenter and work was begun. First, though, the carpenter built a small shack to live in and to store his tools while the church was being built.

As the work progressed, the carpenter told Mabel that by the end of the month he would have to have some money or he wouldn't be able to continue the work. 360,000 Japanese yen—one thousand American dollars—was the sum.

Mabel felt like Jesus' disciple Peter as he was sinking in the sea. "Lord," she prayed, "I don't know how to get that money, but don't let me sink now. I am out of the boat. I have started."

At the end of the month, Mabel found herself counting out the money into the carpenter's hand. All 360,000 Japanese yen, yen by yen. Quite a stack of money! Just where it all had come from, Mabel would have been hard put to tell, but there it was!

What a joy it was when the building was finished to be able to invite the suffering, hopeless people of Hiroshima to come and hear the good news of Christ.

At the very first meeting, the big church was packed. At the close, the people flocked down the aisle to the altar seeking God, the only one who had the answer to their needs.

One of the seekers that evening was a girl from a high-class family who had been terribly burned during the blast of the atomic bomb. Because of her appearance she had not been going out in public.

However, a Christian friend persuaded her to come to the church that evening. "We will sit in the back row, and before the benediction is pronounced I will go out with you," the friend promised.

Before the message was over, the light of God had come into that girl's heart. At the end of the meeting she made her way to the altar with the others. No matter her scarred face!

"I never thought I would ever thank God, or anybody, for these scars," she said, looking up through her tears, "but tonight, in the depths of my being, I thought that if this had not happened to me, I might never have heard this wonderful message about God."

The young woman died not long after that.

When the meeting was over and nearly everyone had gone, Mabel noticed a little woman standing to one side who seemed to be wanting to say something. Mabel went to her and took her hand.

"Oh, Sensei! I understood it! I got it!" the woman exclaimed. And then she told Mabel her story.

"That morning when the bomb struck, I was at my home, up on the mountainside. My two little children were playing on the floor—a one-year-old and a three-year-old.

"I stooped to pick up something, and in that second, that awful flash of light came! I was startled, and stood up to look around. When I looked back, my two children were charred at my feet. Both dead.

"I didn't know then that I was all burned, I was so concerned for my little ones.

"I picked them up and laid them aside, and pretty soon I began to feel the pain in my own body. Then I found how badly I was burned.

"I thought to myself, 'What terrible thing have I done that this should happen to me? And what of my children, who were here just a minute ago. Now they are not!'

"Oh, how I have suffered. I have dragged my weary body to every shrine and every temple I could find. If I would hear of another I would go. But nothing has brought me any comfort. I still did not know where the life of my children had gone.

"But tonight you told us of this God's love, and that it was He who created us, and you said my children are with Him. I believe it! I believe it! My heart is comforted. Light has come to me!"

This woman soon became a faithful member of the church. Because of her burns she endured unimaginable suffering. At one time the sores were infested with maggots because she had no bandages. Finally her eyes were affected, and a doctor told her there was no hope because of the aftereffect of the atomic radiation.

She came to talk with Mr. Oye. "Even though the doctor said there is no help for me, I believe God who could save me can heal this! I want you to pray for me."

Mr. Oye prayed. Within three days she was completely healed, and had no trouble after that.

In order to continue the good work that was going on in Hiroshima there would need to be a Bible school to train more Christian workers. The elder Mr. Oye was an excellent teacher, one of the best Mabel had ever met, and he was willing to help with such a school. But where could it be held? Mabel looked all over for a house to rent that could serve as a school building.

One night as she lay awake, unable to sleep for thinking about the need, God showed her what to do. There was the shack that the carpenter had built. Though it was small, it had two stories. And there was the little house that Mr. Oye lived in while a larger one was being built. Put them together, and there was a school building.

So that is what they did, and the school was begun. The boys' dormitory was upstairs and the girls' downstairs. Both Mr. Oye and his son were teachers.

"This will never do!" a director of the mission exclaimed as he surveyed the makeshift quarters when at last the Alliance returned to Japan in 1949. But they had served the purpose very well all that time.

13

Meeting Needs/ Filling the Emptiness

THE years following the war found the Japanese more open to the message of the Christian gospel than ever before. The national defeat, the destruction of their beautiful cities, the terrible suffering they had endured, and the disclosure that their emperor was not a god after all left them with nothing to hold on to. They were at the point where they were desperately searching for something to fill the awful void.

A Japanese young man who was looking for the living God told Mabel his story.

"About the time I became old enough to think for my self, the teaching of our schools was controlled by war propaganda. Then the war ended and all was lost. All that I had been taught was shattered.

"I felt crazed. I wanted to do everything that was bad. I was so disobedient and profligate that I even beat my old father and mother.

"I got to the end of my rope. One night in my misery, I climbed the mountain near my home. I stood there and screamed out at the moon, but there was no help. I cried out to the forest, but only the echo of my own voice came back.

"Then I thought of the church. I did not know about God, but I thought I would go to the church anyway. I waited until no one was looking and entered secretly and tried to pray. I did not know to whom I was praying but my heart became quiet.

"I went home and apologized to my parents. They said, 'We have waited for this day,' and they wept for joy.

"I determined to be a true man. I did not know Jesus, but I made a wooden cross and put it on my desk and tried to do right.

"Now you tell me of the living Christ. This, oh, this is what I have waited for!"

And this was what the missionaries had been praying and waiting for.

Both Anne and Mabel were regularly getting calls to come to speak to one group or another. Anne, probably because she had been a teacher, was often called to speak to the elite men. She seemed to understand how to reach them with the gospel.

Ever since Mabel had come to Japan all those many years ago, the women of Japan had held a special place in her heart. The years since the end of the war had deepened her love and concern for them. How valiantly they struggled to keep their families alive, scrimping and scraping to keep them fed and clothed and in some semblance of health. How heartening was the loyalty and faithfulness of the Christian women in standing by the work of God, some of them even taking training to serve more effectively.

Calls came from all over the province asking Mabel to come and lecture on such subjects as education and democracy, which served as a springboard for her to present the solution to the problems of post-war Japan—Jesus Christ Himself. There got to be so many requests that the government appointed an official to travel with her and plan and prepare for the meetings. The official would come and get her, take her bag, and escort her personally to the place where she was scheduled to speak.

She traveled to nearly every section of the province and found herself in some surprising circumstances.

In one place where there was no public meeting place, a Buddhist priest invited her to speak in the temple.

Because Mabel was so short that her audience couldn't see her, the priest pulled out his desk and had her stand on that to proclaim the gospel of Christ to her audience—many of them the priest's own people.

What a privilege these opportunities were to minister to the spiritually hungry people of Japan! It got to be that Mabel could hardly step outside without someone running to meet her. When she got on the train, someone was sure to say, "Hello, here she is!" and everyone would nod.

Going to see a friend in the hospital would stretch into a lengthy visit as other patients recognized her and wanted her to pray for them. To Mabel this was a precious ministry.

Anne and Mabel lived for four years in that one little room that had been the only place available when they had first come to Matsuyama. They had kept so busy with their work that they hadn't really thought about their own needs.

One day Mabel fell and hurt her side so badly that she was laid up in bed for several days. While she was recovering, God spoke to her.

It was time now to build her own house.

Build a house? But she had no money.

No matter. He would take care of that. She was to see to building the house; He would see to the money.

What could Mabel do but call a carpenter?

As to where to build the house, Mabel thought she would have to hunt for a piece of land, but the pastor of the church suggested that she build on the church property. There was plenty of room, she wouldn't have to pay taxes, and being close by the church would be much more convenient for her.

Plans were drawn and the house—a good-sized one—was begun. Just at this time, a woman whom Mabel had met years before in Minnesota sent a thousand dollars. What an encouragement that was! And so it went—every time a bill came in, money came in from somewhere.

When the house was finished there was not a penny of debt on it. Everything was paid for.

And how wonderful to be able to go from room to room. "Isn't it lovely to be able to stand in one room and look into another?" Mabel would exclaim.

Not only did they now have a spacious home,

but the house also became headquarters for much of their teaching ministry, both English classes and Bible classes for women. There were two parlors downstairs where Anne and Mabel could each hold a class at the same time, or the parlors could be opened up to make room for one large class.

Upcountry, in Minara, about an hour's train ride from Matsuyama, a small gospel work had been started. Besides the village, there was a big tuberculosis hospital with about 3,000 patients. The pastor in Matsuyama had been taking time out from his work for a cottage prayer meeting there, but Mabel began to feel that there should be a separate work in the village.

One morning one of the Christians brought Mabel the news that a fine piece of land could be purchased reasonably. After looking it over, they bought it.

By the time they were ready to put a building on the property, however, they discovered that it wasn't large enough.

Now what to do?

After a time a man who in lived in another village came with an offer.

"I am not a Christian," he said, "but I own some land, and I want a church up here. I have perceived that wherever there is a Christian church, the standard of the community rises, and I want a church in our village."

He offered to exchange for a very nominal price a larger piece of land for the first property. The trade was made and building began.

Next came a vision for a new ministry: a kindergarten. Since the American occupation, the missionaries had been troubled about changes in educating the children and young people of Japan. Though all of the old Japanese legends were taken out of the school books, the theory of evolution taught as a scientific fact replaced them.

Oh, why couldn't there have been some mention of the God who created the heavens and the earth, Christians agonized. The Japanese were left without any standard, nothing to hold on to.

Students would come with tears streaming down their cheeks. "Sensei, what's the meaning of life, anyhow? I have a good mind, I get good marks, I will graduate with honors and get a good job. I will have a home and children. But then what? Is it worth it all? Maybe I had better snuff out my life now!"

One woman took her son to his teacher because of his disobedience and disrespect at home. The teacher went to the principal with the mother's request for guidance and help.

"You can talk to her only of righteousness," the principal told her.

"Sir, I do not know what righteousness is. We have no standard," the teacher said sadly.

Fortunately, the mother brought her unruly son to the missionaries, who were able to give her the standard from God's Word.

A kindergarten where little children could be taught the things of God day after day, before they entered the primary schools, would at least provide a foundation that families could build on.

Miraculously and marvelously the money began to come in for the kindergarten. Soon there was enough for a building. Young Japanese Christian women were hired to teach and the kindergarten ministry began.

It wasn't long before grateful parents began to pour out their appreciation for the kindergarten.

"When my little boy was born," one father said, "I made up my mind that I would try to teach him respect if it took my lifetime. When the kindergarten opened, I thought that it might be a help, so I sent my small son. After he had been attending the classes for a short time, we were sitting down as usual for our evening meal. I picked up my chopsticks and began to eat.

"'Father, just a minute,' the little fellow said, laying his chopsticks down. Then he bowed his head and thanked God for his food.

"You will never know how much that has meant to me. I thought it would take my whole lifetime to teach him reverence, but he has learned it already!"

A mother told of the intervention of her five-year-old son during an argument between her and the boy's father.

"Forgiving one another! Forgiving one another!" he interrupted, quoting a Bible verse he had learned in kindergarten.

By the time Mabel and Anne left Japan, 93 lively little children were enrolled in the school.

"There is a better way than you have known" was Mabel's message in those dark days after the war, just as it had been when she first arrived in Japan. "Put your faith in Him, the living and true God, and the meaning of existence will no longer be a puzzle to you!"

And besides words, the Japanese had seen the gospel of Christ demonstrated as she helped them put together their broken lives. Even the nation's highest officials were aware of the contribution to their country of the little American missionary.

In 1962 Mabel was given a great honor by the Japanese government. At a special convocation called by the governor himself, Mabel found herself in the presence of representatives of the Emperor.

In an impressive ceremony she was presented with a parchment scroll bearing the Emperor's seal and detailing her service to the Japanese people. A gold medal conferred upon her the unique honor of membership in the highly exclusive Fifth Order of the Sacred Treasure. No foreigner had ever before received such an award. Not even a Japanese citizen had ever been so honored while still living. And now she herself was considered a Japanese citizen.

Mabel could scarcely believe what was happening. "Why have I been chosen?" she asked herself.

But in the words of the governor there was no question as to the appropriateness of honoring this American missionary. "She gave both materially and spiritually to the welfare of the Japanese people," he said, "especially at the close of the war in the time of defeat when the Japanese people were in extreme distress and bewilderment. She traveled widely and gave unprecedented assistance and encouragement to our people by her Christian faith."

14

A Farewell and a Welcome

FOR many years Anne and Mabel were known as "The Ladies" among their many Japanese friends. During 1964, they began to think they should be described as "The Weary Ladies." By that time Anne had been on the field for forty-two years, and Mabel fifty-five.

Anne in those years had mastered the Japanese language and was considered an authority even by the Japanese themselves. She was a well-respected teacher and taught in the Bible school in Hiroshima.

Finally, though, the teaching became too much for her and she returned to live with Mabel and helped launch the church and kindergarten in Minara.

One day she slipped and fell on the polished kindergarten floor and broke her arm. It was a bad break from which she never did really recover, though she was not willing for it to slow her down.

"What's a little broken arm?" she would reply when someone would try to get her to take it easy. But gradually her health declined.

Besides the problem with her arm she had heart trouble, which continued to worsen. Many nights she couldn't seem to get her breath. Mabel too had a heart condition, and they spent many a night praying together.

Finally, they went to Kyoto for a vacation, two ailing elderly ladies, praying for deliverance from their physical problems.

When they asked the Japanese to pray for them, the Japanese would say, "Why, yes, we will pray for you, but don't forget your age!"

No use to depend on their prayers, Mabel decided. They were looking at wrinkles instead of God. But she didn't give up, reassured by the experience of Sarah in the Old Testament. Old age didn't prevent God from fulfilling His promise through her!

However, Mabel became so ill that the doctor said, "If we can't stop this, it is going to stop you!"

Mabel continued to trust. "Your Word cannot fail. It cannot fail! That's all there is to it. I am healed!" she reminded the Lord—and herself.

She regained her health. The same could not be said for Anne, whose health continued to decline during 1965.

One morning, the Lord spoke to Mabel: "You must now get ready to go home and take her away. This is too much for her."

Mabel had always dreaded the day when she would have to leave Japan. How could she ever stand it? Surely she would weep and weep.

But an amazing thing happened. Suddenly she was filled with an amazing sense of God's peace. Not one tear did she shed. It was all right! She set to work packing and disposing of items to be discarded. All by herself—because Anne, by now, was unable to help—Mabel got ready to return to the States for good.

Quite a stir came about when the Japanese in Matsuyama found out that the American ladies were actually going to leave.

There were radio and television interviews, which gave Mabel an opportunity to speak to thousands who never would have entered a church. The prospect was quite overwhelming.

"I feel like Samson," Mabel remarked. "He killed more Philistines in his death than during his life. Now it seems that God is allowing me to reach more people through my retiring than during my lifetime of ministry."

At an impressive ceremony held in the largest auditorium in town and attended by government dignitaries from Ehime Prefecture and representatives from the Lions, Rotary and Women's clubs, the mayor himself presented Mabel with the key to the city. "For your love and work toward the promotion of social welfare with great sacrifice," he said, "the people of Matsuyama confer upon you, Miss R. Mabel Francis, the title of Special Honorary Citizen of Matsuyama."

This was a great honor, Mabel realized: the greatest tribute a city can bestow upon a person. Be that as it may, she was later to reminisce to one of her fellow missionaries that God had given her the key to the city long ago.

In response to the mayor's presentation, Mabel promised to continue her work of bridging the gap between Japan and America through Christian friendship and service.

Later in the program, when Mabel was asked to speak, she poured out her heart to impress upon her audience God's great love that had brought missionaries to Japan in the first place and had kept them there all through the years.

A thousand students from the Shinomome Christian School were present, and the girls' choir gave a beautiful rendition of the "Hallelujah Chorus" in English. At the end of the ceremony the crowd, with tears flowing, sang "God Be With You 'Til We Meet Again."

The Japanese Christians were thrilled with Mabel's witness at the ceremony. They had been praying for just such an opportunity. God had been truly glorified.

Though Anne had been in Matsuyama only a few years compared to Mabel's forty-six, she, too, was honored.

Mabel had several more opportunities to remind Japanese officials and leaders of God's great love for them. "God has created you, the Japanese nation. There is no other people like you. You are a peculiar nation, and God has an intense love for you. He has a purpose for you. The reason Japan is hemmed in on these little islands is because you haven't the love that goes out and loves the world," she told them. "If only the Japanese loved God, what they could do for the world!"

All of the missionaries and churches in the area

also had services of farewell for Anne and Mabel.

Then came the day of the departure, September 6, 1965. Hundreds were at the airport to see the missionary sisters off.

Their destination was Toledo, Ohio. Tom had lived there until his death and they had spent a short furlough there in 1962. Just what they would do when they got there, they had no idea, but the Lord would provide, they were sure.

A crowd of friends and well-wishers was awaiting their arrival in Toledo, and there was a lovely time of greeting and fellowship.

Finally it was time to say good night, but the new arrivals weren't abandoned to find themselves a place to sleep. They were carried off to the home of Mr. and Mrs. George McLean, where a comfortable basement apartment had been prepared for them. It was not just a stopover, but a home where they could spend the rest of their days if they wished. There would be only a small monthly charge for utilities, but never any rent to pay. The cupboards and refrigerator had been stocked with food by friends from the church. The beds were made up, and, to make the welcome complete, there was a vase of red rosebuds. What a homecoming!

Those weeks of fall and early winter, Anne's health continued to fail. She spent a great deal of time in prayer for the work in Japan and the loved ones there.

Just after Christmas, on December 28, Anne and Mabel had a particularly precious time praying together, and Anne seemed brighter and stronger. During lunch they were reading letters when Anne suddenly collapsed and fell to the floor.

Mabel rushed to her, but she was gone.

"Like Enoch," Mabel was to describe Anne's departure later, "she did not see death. She opened her eyes and it was heaven."

15

Still On Call

ANYONE who had been expecting Mabel Francis to actually retire and take it easy for the rest of her days would have found themselves quite mistaken.

On the plane coming home from Japan, God had given her a new commission: To tell the people at home what she had learned through the years about living one life with Him.

Soon her calendar was being filled with speaking engagements, which eventually took her from coast to coast. This little old lady in her nineties had something that people—Christians and non-Christians alike—wanted and needed, were hungering and thirsting for. Perhaps not everybody could have put it into words, but as the Japanese had discovered, here was the life of Christ being lived out in an ordinary person.

She made a deep impression on those who heard her speak at a Life Investment Conference for young people of the Christian and Missionary Alliance.

"A livin' doll!" a television news reporter called her.

"Bring that young man back," she said when she heard what he had said. "Tell him that I'm an old war horse, with still a lot to get done for the Lord!"

And so she did.

Somehow she found the time to write a book, *One Shall Chase a Thousand*, which, besides being a spiritual journal of God's dealings with her from early childhood, details her missionary work.

In 1969 came a wonderful opportunity to return with her niece Ida for a five-month visit to Japan. The occasion for going was the celebration of the twentieth anniversary of the reestablished Alliance Church.

Everywhere they went, they were met by Japanese friends bearing flowers and greetings. In the province where Mabel had lived they were greeted by the governor himself and rode in his limousine (lace curtains and all!).

While Ida was sightseeing, Mabel visited her Japanese friends and spoke in many of the churches. Ida, too, did some speaking. Being a teacher of reading in the States, she claimed the intense interest of the Japanese. She was even invited to appear on Japanese television to tell about her home and her work in America.

As it turned out, the visit stretched to a full ten months, and even that wasn't enough for Mabel whose heart still burned with love for the Japanese people. "Oh, the need I felt," she wrote. "Had I been younger, nothing could have induced me to leave."

When Mr. Oye, who came to know the Lord through Mabel's ministry and later became the

Japanese representative of the Christian and Missionary Alliance, was invited to the States for a series of meetings, Mabel traveled with him as his interpreter. With her nieces Gladys and Ida they went sightseeing, including a tour of Washington, D.C., for their Japanese guest.

In February of 1972, Mabel had another opportunity to travel, this time to Hawaii. The trip was arranged by Ellis and Virginia Roth of Grabill, Indiana. Virginia had grown up in the Toledo area and had been a missionary in Hawaii for a number of years. She would accompany Mabel. Her vision was for Mabel to minister to the many older Japanese there. Mabel was eager to go. No matter that she would soon be ninety-two years of age.

One of the first meetings was with the ministerial association in Honolulu. After hearing Mabel, the ministers invited her to come and speak in their churches.

It turned out to be a pretty heavy schedule, but Mabel didn't mind. She got tired, yes, and sometimes her voice would almost give out, but a little rest would rejuvenate her.

She was pleased to be able to minister to the Japanese in their own language. There were two large meetings of Japanese. Although most of them understood English, they appreciated hearing their native tongue. She spoke not only to the older Japanese, but to people of all ages, other nationalities and different denominations.

All in all it was a blessed, if busy, month. Mabel had not gone to Hawaii as a vacationing tourist. Being able to tell others of the joy of knowing her heavenly Father was her delight.

For some time Mabel had been aware that something was going to have to be done about a sore on her lip that had been troubling her for six years. Upon her return to the mainland the doctor pronounced that the growth was malignant and would have to be removed as soon as possible.

Of course, she had been praying about the matter and trusted that the Lord would heal her as He had so many times through the years. This time, however, it appeared that He was going to use surgery to accomplish the healing. To those who wondered that she hadn't been healed already, she said, "Don't be stumbled. God has His way. He knows best."

A surgeon who shared Mabel's trust in the Lord took over the case, and she went confidently to surgery. So relaxed was she that she actually fell asleep after the pinprick of the needle for the anesthetic, which was only a local. She woke up when the doctor gave her a shake to tell her she was back in her room.

The surgery did not heal as quickly as Mabel and the doctor had hoped. Her mouth had taken on a little sidewise twist and was a bit undependable when eating and drinking. Finally, late in the fall of 1973, more surgery had to be performed to take care of the problem.

It was a time of suffering, but there were blessings,

too. Among them was seeing God supply her needs financially.

After Medicare had paid its share of the bill, $800 remained to be paid. Mabel had on hand just four dollars.

"Lord, you know all about it," she said.

Of course He did. From here and there money came in—over a thousand dollars!

"So I was richer than when I started," Mabel said with a chuckle, when telling about it later.

After the second surgery she found herself feeling alarmingly weak. No strength, but things to do and places to go!

Well, maybe.

She sought God's will as to what her ministry should be now and perhaps for the rest of her life, however long that might be. Could it be that her public ministry was ending?

An experience occurred to her mind that had happened years ago in Japan. She had been working in her kitchen when a voice said clearly, "Go to your room and read Psalm 110."

Mabel obeyed.

"The LORD said unto my Lord, Sit thou at my right hand, until I make thine enemies thy footstool," the first verse read.

In her mind's eye, Mabel could see the Mighty Conqueror sitting as Victor, waiting until the last foe is put down. And, according to Ephesians 2:6, here she was, seated with Him, already living the victory that Christ had come to give each of His children.

Mabel wrote in her 1972 Christmas letter: "What a glorious life! Not seeking to enter, but living in His patience, waiting with Him. I long to be able to tell all what this means to me. Oh, to give a word that will tell of this glorious life of victory before I leave this old world—something that will lead others to cast all aside and just live for Him!"

Life physically, now, was having more downs than ups. Early in 1973 Mabel moved to Shell Point Village, a Christian and Missionary Alliance retirement community in Fort Myers, Florida. At first she had her own apartment.

During this time Mabel wrote the booklet *Filled With the Spirit . . . Then What?* in which she expands upon her experiences in dealing with the problem of self.

On her 93rd birthday, July 26, feeling quite well, though still not as strong as she would have liked, she was honored with a special reception at the Village.

As the summer wore on, Mabel became weaker and weaker. Finally she was transferred to the Nursing Pavilion where with special care, rest, and nutritious meals she regained her strength. Soon she was up and about, being a blessing and an encouragement to the other residents of Shell Point Village.

In a letter written in May 1974, Mabel tells of being very ill: "Went to death's door, but just when all hope seemed gone, I heard His voice saying, 'I still have work for you on earth,' and from that moment I began to get better. I am still not quite well, but tire easily. I must get stronger."

She closes the letter with this poem (author unknown):

> My goal is God Himself, not joy nor peace,
> Nor even blessing, but Himself, my God;
> Tis His to lead me there, not mine but His—
> "At any cost, dear Lord, by any road."

For about a year she was able to carry on the work God had for her. Then on Monday, May 12, 1975, as she was walking down the hall of the Nursing Pavilion after ministering to a very ill friend, she felt something snap in her right hip. She couldn't move her foot, and holding the rail along the hall, she slowly sank to the floor. The resident doctor and a nurse were immediately on hand to help her. She was sent to the hospital in Fort Myers and put in the care of an orthopedist.

It was a broken hip, of course, and a metal hip replaced the broken one. The day following surgery, Mabel was walking around her room. The doctor was pleased with her steady progress and in ten days she was dismissed from the hospital.

For some time, Mabel had been looking forward to the visit of two Japanese pastors who were coming as delegates to the 1975 General Council of the Christian and Missionary Alliance. The visitors were Rev. Tamura of Hiroshima, President of the Japan National Christian Church, and Rev. Kuwabara, Pastor of the Matsuyama church. They had been dear fellow workers for many years and now once again she was able to enjoy fellowship with them as they came to visit her at Shell Point Village. Such a precious time it was that after they left she declared contentedly, "Now I am ready for Jesus to take me home."

After her return from the hospital to the Nursing Pavilion, some of her friends took turns keeping her company night and day so that she was never left alone, and they ministered to her every need.

She followed her doctor's orders and every day did some walking. She was regaining her strength very nicely.

On June 6, she took two walks and seemed stronger than at any other time since her mishap.

Early in the morning of June 7, Miss Deanna Coppec, who stayed every night from eleven p.m. until seven a.m., noted a change in Mabel's breathing. The nurse and doctor were called and oxygen administered. Slowly, slowly her heart was weakening, and she fell into a deep sleep.

Shortly after noon Mabel opened her eyes, smiled, and lifted her fingers in farewell. Then, with no apparent pain or struggle of any kind, she was in the presence of her Lord.